ARTIST'S MARKET
BUSINESS SERIES

HOW TO MAKE YOUR DESIGN BUSINESS PROFITABLE

Joyce M. Stewart

NORTH
LIGHT
BOOKS

Cincinnati, Ohio

How to Make Your Design Business Profitable. Copyright © 1992 by Joyce M. Stewart. Printed and bound in the United States of America. All rights reserved. No part of this book may be reproduced in any form or by any electronic or mechanical means including information storage and retrieval systems without permission in writing from the publisher, except by a reviewer, who may quote brief passages in a review. Published by North Light Books, an imprint of F&W Publications, Inc., 1507 Dana Avenue, Cincinnati, Ohio 45207; 1(800)289-0963. First edition.

96   95   94   93   92   5   4   3   2   1

Library of Congress Cataloging in Publication Data

Stewart, Joyce M.
  How to make your design business profitable / Joyce M. Stewart. — 1st ed.
      p.   cm. — (Artist's market business series)
  Includes bibliographical references and index.
  ISBN 0-89134-391-1 (paper)
  1. Design services—United States—Management—Handbooks, manuals, etc. 2. Design services—United States—Marketing—Handbooks, manuals, etc. I. Title. II. Series.
NK1403.S74   1992
745.4'068—dc20   91-26892
                                                                CIP

Concept and editorial direction by: Diana Martin
Designed by: Carol Buchanan

To Mark Fishbein, a true friend and a nimble editor.

ACKNOWLEDGMENTS
My largest debt in writing this book is to the designers and businesspeople who so generously shared their insights with me. Their explorations of the points at which design and business intersect were invaluable. I also thank Laurel Harper for planting the book's seed, and Diana Martin and Susan Conner for tending its growth. Mark Fishbein, Emily Cohen, Jim Walters, Carlo Adinolfi and Christian Waters supplied me with loyal support and expert advice from the beginning to the end of this endeavor.

ABOUT THE AUTHOR
Joyce M. Stewart is a freelance journalist and fiction writer who lives in New York City. She is the regular business columnist for *HOW* magazine, and her work has been published in a variety of national magazines and newsletters.

CONTENTS

CHAPTER 3
GETTING PAID . . . WELL AND ON TIME 26

Price your jobs profitably and get paid on time by:
- Knowing how to set (and raise) standard job rates.
- Getting what you want during negotiation.
- Keeping the usage rights you need to reap future financial benefits.
- Bringing in money faster while retaining your clients' good will.
- Stressing the benefits of immediate payment.
- Dealing with clients who don't pay.

CHAPTER 4
KEEP THE CASH FLOWING 46

Capitalize on the strength of every dollar you make by:
- Recognizing your true "financial" colors.
- Keeping track of where your money comes from and where it goes.
- Choosing the right accounting method.
- Knowing when to spend money to make money.

CHAPTER 5
TAX-SLASHING STRATEGIES 64

There are many simple (and legal) ways to pay Uncle Sam less than you did last year by:
- Keeping good records.
- Maximizing your deductions.
- Estimating your taxes correctly to avoid penalties.
- Avoiding audits, or knowing how to deal with them.

CHAPTER 6

PROMOTING YOUR STUDIO EFFECTIVELY 80

Make the right impression and generate more business by:
- Pinpointing the right prospects.
- Spending your promotional dollars wisely on cost-effective promotions.
- Spotting new marketing opportunities right under your nose.
- Realizing the long-term value of free work for a good cause.

CHAPTER 7

HOW TO MAKE CLIENT-WINNING PRESENTATIONS 92

How to win the clients you want by:
- Communicating clearly, on paper and in person.
- Choosing visuals that will attract and keep your client's attention.
- Customizing your presentations for prospective clients.
- Tackling and overcoming common obstacles to effective selling.

CHAPTER 8
MANAGING YOUR STAFF EFFECTIVELY

Build a solid team by:
- Knowing when you need extra help.
- Using hiring methods that guarantee you'll get the right people.
- Letting your staff know when they're on (and off) track.
- Setting clear, achievable goals for meaningful progress.
- Setting salaries that won't break the budget.
- Knowing when letting someone go is in your best interest.

CHAPTER 9
USING PROFESSIONAL SERVICES WISELY

Save yourself thousands of dollars in mistakes *not made* by:
- Getting legal advice up front.
- Finding accountants and tax planners to manage your finances.
- Hiring a bookkeeper.
- Knowing where to find answers to special business problems.

RESOURCES
Here are organizations and publications that will help you manage your business better.

INDEX

INTRODUCTION

I began this book with the belief that, fundamentally, design ability and business sense don't really mix. During the year it took me to write it, I learned that designers have a lot more business sense than I ever dreamed, and that what they don't know, they are hungry to learn. My concept of the recondite artist who can't be bothered with the mundane concern of turning a profit has evaporated forever.

This book is a straightforward guide to running a profitable design business. While I was pleasantly surprised by the business savvy I found in many designers, even the most astute admitted that there were some aspects of running a business that left them completely baffled. I hope this book will serve as a primer for all designers, to help them with the facets of business in which they need guidance.

The opening chapter of this book should help you set up and monitor your studio's financial progress. The next two chapters deal with time management and pricing jobs, both of which are essential to making a profit in the design field. Following are chapters on billing, accounting and taxes—the financial nuts and bolts of your business. After the number-crunching section, two chapters cover the marketing and self-promotion efforts required to make your studio grow and prosper. I've included a chapter on cost-effective staffing, and, finally, the last chapter shows you where to look for professional advice.

Most designers open their own studios for two reasons: They want greater artistic freedom and heftier profits than a salaried design job can typically offer. In the course of writing this book, I have observed a fascinating, oft-repeated progression: When a design business is well managed, its profits rise, and those incremental earnings eventually provide the designer with even more room for taking artistic chances. This new-found artistic freedom results in even more creative design work, which in turn brings even greater recognition and more business to the studio. The key to launching your studio on this upward spiral lies in first managing its bottom line. This book can help you make your design business more profitable. As for the use you make of the greater artistic freedom that results from your increased profits, well, that's up to you!

—Joyce M. Stewart

CHAPTER 1

RUNNING A PROFITABLE STUDIO

PROFIT POINTS

Make a comfortable profit in the lean years as well as the good ones by:

- Establishing an effective business plan.
- Cutting overhead costs to boost the bottom line.
- Making the smartest investments in studio upgrades.
- Knowing when to buy equipment that can make you more money.

Whether you're setting up your first studio or have been in business for decades, there are ways to run your studio more profitably. Although watching costs and focusing on more lucrative projects can be extremely important to your bottom line, decisions about how your studio is set up or about which expansions to make can also have a significant impact on your profit margin. This chapter will help you make those kinds of decisions wisely, so you can maintain a comfortable profit in the lean years as well as the good ones.

WRITING AND USING A BUSINESS PLAN

Before you even put pencil to sketchpad on your studio's first design project, you should have a fully developed and documented *business plan*. No other single document will be more important to help focus your ideas into a well-thought-out plan to guide your studio's day-to-day operation, management and future. Contrary to what some people think, a business plan is not a useless formality; it is an important road map that states what your business is all about, where it's going, and how you plan on taking it there. The business plan is also a guideline for cost and profit watching, providing an excellent source of information about your company's financial health and your ability to expand profitably.

Your business plan should do the following:

- Define the mission statement of your business.
- Clearly and quantitatively state your business goals and objectives.
- Focus your future goals on your studio's growth.
- Provide a profile of what your business is all about.
- Keep track of how day-to-day activities will help you reach those goals.
- Provide an analysis of your competition.
- Provide an analysis of your marketing strategy and approach.
- Highlight the best growth areas for your studio.
- Outline sound financial planning to project capital and revenues.

In short, a good business plan allows you to see clearly (and to explain to others) what your studio is all about and where it is going professionally and financially, to anticipate potholes in the road to success, and to make wise decisions about allocating your firm's resources.

When preparing a business plan, remember to document the facts that support your goals and decisions. You may understand a concept or situation, but don't forget that others may not. Explain clearly why you have set your goals and how you plan to accomplish them. This also demonstrates your professional thoroughness.

Be sure your goals are financially ambitious, but realistic. Look carefully at projected sales and cash flow, and make sure they are reasonable. Ask yourself what would happen if sales were to total 20 percent less than you expected. If the whole plan would crumble, you may be playing it too close to the edge.

It's always good practice to get an objective opinion of your plan. Ask your accountant or other business advisor to help you formulate reasonable and accurate business projections. There are also several software packages on the market designed to help you write a business plan. They tabulate projections using the numbers you plug in for your business, and even provide text for the written part of the plan (e.g., "Based on the initial capital investment of $x for the new x equipment, we expect our second-year profits to be x percent of total sales generated, or $x.") Just reading through the text of business plan software can help familiarize you with the issues and questions to be covered in a thorough, effective business plan. Check with your local software dealer for specific business plan packages. Most are

MAKING YOUR PLAN COMPLETE

Although your studio's business plan is a written report, it is a living document. As such, it should be updated at least once a year (or more often if dramatic changes take place in your business or the economy). Your business plan should contain the following sections:

Executive Summary. This is probably the most important and most often read section of the business plan. As a summary of the entire plan, it is an overview of your studio and its potential. Describe your goals for the next year, how you plan to achieve them, and what the financial return on your monetary investment is expected to be. This section should appear either first or last in your business plan. Remember, this is an all inclusive summary of the entire plan. Even if you plan on placing it first, it is important to write it last, after you have completed the financial information contained in other sections.

Table of Contents. Since most people won't read a business plan cover to cover, and a bank officer will read it for entirely different reasons than a potential partner would, readers have to know exactly where the sections they're interested in can be found.

Mission Statement. This is a one or two sentence statement of what your business is all about, what you believe your mission is. It should be as quantifiable as possible. For example, you might state your mission this way: To create a medium-size, self-sufficient graphic design studio that will operate at a 10 percent net profit margin.

Background and studio goals. This section should be a brief overview of where you've been and where you are planning to go. Give both past and projected sales figures, describe how your design philosophy and types of projects have evolved over the years, and

outline where you'd like the business to be in one, five and ten years. Include sales figures, new markets to explore, the profitability of past projects, and changes in the design market. Although you can use the past to clarify and inform, your focus should be on the future.

Current goals. This portion should present more detail than the previous section on the main goals you are working toward now, what the costs will be in achieving them, and when you expect to realize a profit.

Situation Analysis. State all of the factors that influenced your choice of current and future goals, as well as the factors you believe will influence your success. Describe the demand for your designs and how it is changing, your target markets, your competition, advantages your studio can provide versus that of the competition, any legal restrictions, and all other variables that are important to the successful achievement of your goals. Be optimistic, but realistic.

Market Strategy. You must differentiate your studio from your competitors. Detail who you will market to and why, and what self-promotion strategies you plan to use. Also include an itemized marketing budget under this category.

Financial plans. This section is the financial heart of your business plan; you should have your accountant, attorney or business manager help prepare it. Include an income statement, a cash flow statement and a balance sheet, each with projections of at least two years. (See Chapter Four for information on what these statements are and how to prepare them.)

An Implementation Schedule. Estimate when each of the steps toward your larger goal will be accomplished, and use this schedule to check your progress monthly or on a regular basis.

priced between $100 and $200 and are usually IBM or Macintosh compatible.

Think of your business plan as the one document you can always reach for to bring your business back into focus. Too often when a business is starting out, or when spending seems out of control, you'll be tempted to take on any client or type of work just to bring the dollars in. This single act can lead you into a downward spiral. Suddenly your design business is not what you imagined it would be — financially or aesthetically. Your business plan can guide your business back to what you want it to be and remind you of the financial realities that will help turn it around.

HOW TO CUT COSTS

The costs of running a design studio can be large and varied, and are often hard to keep track of. The quickest way to get your studio into trouble is to lose track of expenses, letting them balloon out of control and progressively erode your profits. To explain the true nature of costs and how they affect profitability, we must first differentiate between *fixed* and *variable* costs.

Fixed costs. This category includes all of the unvarying expenditures of your business. How much work you do has no effect on fixed costs. Rent or mortgage payments are fixed costs because you must pay the same amount whether you are working in your studio fifteen hours a day or your drawing tables sit empty for weeks on end. Other fixed costs include insurance, utilities, accounting fees, depreciation, and loan payments. The total of all your fixed costs is called your studio's *overhead*.

Variable costs. These are expenses that do change according to how much work you've done or how much you need to spend. Art supplies are variable costs (for instance, you don't use much paper if you aren't designing, and when you are you can decide what type paper you want to use and how much you want to spend on it), as are freelancer's salaries, most travel expenses, and advertising.

Monitoring Costs Strategically

In a design studio (as in most service businesses) fixed costs make up the bulk of expenditures. For this reason, one of the keys to profitability is to cut overhead costs to the bone and keep them there. The single most common reason businesses fail, especially in their beginning, is that their soaring overhead costs overwhelm their revenues. Following are some suggestions for monitoring and cutting overhead costs:

■ *Keep financial commitments short-term.* Even if a landlord offers you a good deal on a five-year lease, opt for a shorter one, especially if you're just starting up. Don't lock into a fixed cost that may end up costing you your studio. If you have any unused space in the studio location you choose, you may opt to rent it out to another designer. (See the discussion on cooperative studios later in this chapter.)

■ *Keep salaried staff to a minimum.* In general, you don't want more salaried staff than your studio can afford to pay through possible hard times. You want to avoid having to lay off good employees simply because of lack of work (and the accompanying revenues). If business starts to boom, but you're not sure how long it will last (for example, you win a bid on *one* large project, not necessarily a steady account), you're better off using freelancers, whom you can hire on a job-by-job basis. Since salaried staff tend to be more loyal and have more invested in the success of your studio, the decision between hiring a salaried staffer or a freelancer is never easy.

■ *Invest in marketing, not equipment.* It's tempting to buy all the latest technology and the finest in furnishings for your studio because you don't want to seem amateurish. While image is important to a design studio, clients are more important. When money is tight, (especially at start-up) you'll need to focus on getting and keeping clients because of your design abilities, rather than impressing them with technical acquisitions.

PERSONAL PROFILE

BARBARA VOLLMER, Partner
Satogata/Vollmer, Inc.
Cincinnati, Ohio

"A friend of mine who is an attorney and also understands small business finance helped us start off on the right foot," says Barbara Vollmer, partner in the Cincinnati, Ohio, design firm of Satogata/Vollmer, Inc. "He set up a simple financial table that listed our projected first-year expenses on one side and our projected first-year income on the other. As my prospective partner, Frank Satogata, and I started having informal talks with potential clients about what business we might be able to expect from them if we opened our own studio, we would go back to the 'projected income' section of the table and add in the estimated amounts. Each time we had a new 'promise' from a prospective client, we would consult our attorney friend and say, 'Now do we have enough? Is this enough to cover start-up expenses?' He would be encouraging but conservative in urging us to find a few more dollars in projected income before taking the plunge."

Finally, the promise of a major project for the Taft Museum in Cincinnati helped convince Vollmer, her partner, and their attorney that it was finally time to set out on their own. On June 3, 1985, Satogata/Vollmer, Inc. opened its doors for business. Although their studio got off to a terrific start with strong first-year earnings, both partners were thankful for the attorney's conservative estimates when the Taft Museum project fell through. "Without that careful first tally to go back to," Vollmer notes, "I'm sure Frank and I would have panicked when the largest project we had forecasted fell through right after our first year in business. The point is, we had already learned how to set goals and keep tabs on what would be coming in and going out. We had a strong sense of our studio's financial health, so we were able to keep our heads when a major project we had counted on suddenly evaporated."

Six years later, Satogata/Vollmer, Inc. is still going strong. The studio does mostly corporate communications work—annual reports, corporate identities, capabilities brochures—for such corporate giants as the Kroger Company, Chemed Corporation, Penn Central Corporation, Hillenbrand Industries, and the Manhattan National Life Insurance Company. And, yes, even though their first big fish got away, they still do smaller projects for the Taft Museum. Besides Vollmer and her partner, the studio also employs one senior designer.

"Although our clients are for the most part larger corporations, they seem to really enjoy working with a small, less formal studio. When clients come to our studio, which is a huge, open loft space filled with creative interior design and examples of our work, they immediately relax, and can really get into the spirit of working with us creatively while they are here. We find that a relaxed, artistic workspace has *added* to our appeal among these mega-companies rather than making us look less professional," says Vollmer.

■ *Look for the fat in your budget and trim it.* Do you really need three copiers and their huge lease payments? Do you need all of your studio space? Just cutting down slightly on superfluous office equipment, or renting out a corner of your studio with a drawing table and shared use of the receptionist and office facilities, can save you a good amount of money each month.

Lowering overhead is one of the surest ways to enable your studio to survive tough times.

No matter how well you're doing, always keep one thing in mind: Every dollar you save in overhead goes directly into widening your studio's pretax profit margin and insuring its continued success.

Although we've centered our discussion on watching fixed costs, it is important to realize that your variable expenses should be kept to a minimum as well. It is too easy to think of expenses as "all tax deductible in the long run." When times are tough, don't go on a shopping spree with supplies or feel it's okay to bring in

"In some ways, a design business is less risky to start up than another kind of business because it is not a very capital-intensive business. In other words, we didn't have to invest in a large amount of equipment or other expensive overhead to start up," notes Vollmer. "Frank and I both took out small loans to cover start-up costs, which we paid back within the first year we were in business. To this day, I really don't like to borrow any kind of money for our studio. It's just much harder to face the lean times when you know you have a loan payment to meet each month, whether that month has been good for your business or just so-so."

Vollmer still operates with a "no-debt" policy, keeping studio profits in a separate account until she decides where the money should be invested. When the studio invested in a computer system a few years back, Vollmer paid for it in total with the studio's accumulated cash. Now when cash reserves build up, she looks for safe investments such as bank certificates of deposit to invest in.

Although Vollmer keeps a close eye on the studio's financial health, the studio uses an accounting firm (recommended by the "guardian angel" attorney that helped advise them at the start) to prepare quarterly tax and financial statements for them. "For a few thousand dollars a year, it's good to have someone looking over our finances, especially since I don't have any real business or accounting training. It's just comforting to know that all of the numbers will be seen by at least three people. Hopefully one of us will catch any financial missteps," says Vollmer.

a catered lunch every Friday for all of your employees. You'll rob yourself of profits and put your design firm itself in danger.

FINDING THE RIGHT WORKSPACE

A comfortable, creatively designed workspace can do a great deal to inspire you and your employees. Moreover, rent or a mortgage is typically one of your largest overhead expenses. So when you choose a workspace, pay attention to both your creative needs and your financial limitations. Consider the following points and options in looking for and using a workspace for your studio.

Home Studios

For many designers, especially those who run a one-person studio, this is the best situation. To minimize start-up costs, many designers launch their businesses out of a room in their homes. While there are substantial tax advantages to using a home workspace (see Chapter Five), the requirements for deductibility are stringent. Also, many people find it difficult to focus on design work with the distractions of home so close at hand. However, if you are disciplined and focused enough, and if you have a strong need to keep down your overhead costs, you should look into creating a suitable studio space within your home.

Cooperative Studios

This can be the ideal compromise between a drawing table in a spare room at home and a full-fledged commercial workspace of your own. In a cooperative studio, space is shared by several artists who pay rent according to the square footage they occupy. Some cooperatives hire a receptionist or buy communal equipment such as a copier or darkroom facilities and share the costs. Contact your local design industry group for information about design cooperatives in your area.

Making the Best Choice

There are three key things to look for in your studio space: creativity, sufficient space and, of course, cost effectiveness. Look for space that has a creative rather than a corporate atmosphere. Although you want a decent neighborhood and building, don't limit your options by aiming for a purely corporate appearance. Many designers have turned warehouse lofts into creative workspaces that are both funky and functional. Even the most straitlaced clients expect a more laid-back atmosphere in a design studio.

Before signing any agreement, make sure the space you've chosen can be renovated or redesigned according to your specifications.

Zoning laws, poor wiring or drainage systems, and less than solid flooring can stop your interior design plans cold.

Be sure your space includes room for expansion. You might even want to take the extra space and sublease it. Another option is to rent just the space you need with a clause built into your lease that provides for your studio's spatial expansion as your design success grows. Either way, you'll have the space available if and when you decide to buy new equipment or take on additional staff. It's best to allow for expansion room early on; moving your design studio is confusing for clients and costly for you.

Ideally you should create a separate, quiet conference room for client presentations. While a large, open area is great for freelancers or production people, make sure to have some quiet office space set aside for work that requires more privacy. Prefab, portable partitions or decorative room dividers are great options. (These are costs that should be included in your decision when looking for workspace.)

PERSONAL PROFILE

LAURA LAMAR, Partner
MAX
San Francisco, California

For most of us, the San Francisco earthquake of 1989 was a series of nightly newscasts that evoked our sympathy for the disaster's victims. For graphic designer Laura Lamar, it meant the instantaneous ruin of the lovely studio space her design firm, MAX, had called home for the previous four years.

MAX is a small studio specializing in editorial/publication design and illustration. All of its work is done on computer, and the studio employs Lamar and her husband and partner, Max Seabaugh (an illustrator), as well as a graphic designer/art director, several freelancers, and a part-time bookkeeper.

Luckily, both Lamar and MAX landed on their feet. None of the studio employees were hurt in the disaster, but the building was one of the first to be condemned, and it was padlocked shut the day after the earthquake. When Lamar and Seabaugh were finally allowed to enter the building several days later, they didn't even have time to assess the damage. They were given two hours to haul out as much as they could salvage from the wreckage of their studio.

"The damage was mind-boggling," says Lamar. "The studio was in a beautiful brick building dating from 1907. All of the large, arched windows were broken, the plaster was off the walls, tall bookcases were face down on the floor. Flat file drawers had shot across the room, and their contents littered the floor. But, amazingly, none of our computer equipment had been damaged. And since we do all of our design work on computer, most of the work in progress was saved on computer disks, which remained unharmed."

With only a few minutes left inside the condemned building, Lamar and Seabaugh decided to try to move out the high-tech copier they were leasing with an agreement to buy. Even though it wasn't technically theirs, they couldn't bear to abandon it amid the building's rubble. It was the last item they were able to move out of the wrecked space, and their good deed was rewarded in a surprising way. Months later, still sorting out the wreckage of their jumbled business files, they found the leasing agreement for the copier, and discovered that on the very day of the earthquake, the lease contract had terminated and the copier became their studio's property!

Lamar and her partner made appointments with leasing agents the day after the earthquake to look for new studio space. After putting what they could in storage, and working from their apartment and other makeshift workspaces for two months, they moved into a new studio space with one-third more footage and a separate storage closet, something their old space had lacked. And even better, the new building is reinforced and built on a hill of solid rock, so future shocks have less chance of doing serious damage.

"Although we would have never chosen to do things this way, the move was a good thing for us," says Lamar. "We had been growing cramped in our old space, but we had a leasing agreement to stay there for two more

Buying vs. Renting Studio Space

Whether to buy depends on factors such as the condition of the local real estate market, your business's strength, and the stability of the neighborhood. Buying real estate is a large, long-term overhead commitment and one that should be discussed with your accountant or attorney.

COMPUTER DESIGN SYSTEMS

Before the advent of computerized design systems, the most expensive piece of equipment a design studio might consider buying was probably a stat camera. But, faced with a dazzling new array of terrific computerized design programs, more than a few designers have given in to the temptation to have a computer system of their very own. Such systems can increase profits tremendously and open up markets of potential clients you could only daydream about snaring before. For instance, a simple type change can be made with the push of a button, rather than pasting of a whole new mechanical — saving you the time and money such changes usually cost. And since mechanicals are so much easier to create and modify, you can show a potential client a whole new range of options for a job.

Buying vs. Leasing Equipment

Paying for computer equipment, however, can send your studio into bankruptcy if the expenditure turns out to be beyond your means, whether you're shopping for simple Mac software or a $100,000 Light Speed system. So, how do designers decide whether they can afford to upgrade to the latest and greatest or whether they should stick with their current design capabilities and save for the future? Buying a computer design system, or any other large piece of equipment, is a serious financial commitment. But, if you can objectively answer all of the following questions with a Yes, your new equipment will be affordable in the short term, and will be a solid, long-term investment.

■ *In the long run, will the new equipment help me realize more income than it costs?* The goal in using a business loan (or any capital resource) is always to make the investment more than pay for itself by its ability to increase your studio's money-making capacity. If the equipment will save you costs on substantial work you normally job out or will enable you to attract more clients and bigger jobs, the equipment should pay for itself. (See Chapter Four for detailed decision making guidelines for taking on debt.)

years, so we had been just making do. The rent per square foot in our new space is considerably lower, thus lowering our studio's overhead quite a bit, and I don't miss the few amenities we had in our old place that we don't have here. For the most part, they were superfluous anyway."

Lamar and her partner jazzed up the new space with a playful new entranceway that makes use of a three-dimensional MAX logo and a huge floral arrangement in a freestanding, sculptural vase. The large, open room is furnished with the modular furniture, custom-made computer worktops, and computer equipment, which were all salvaged from the old studio.

Even before the studio's "shake up," Lamar was an efficient keeper of business records and a conscientious saver. She feels that the fact that most of the studio's bills had been paid and invoices sent out when the earthquake hit helped to keep a genuine disaster from being even worse. "We had enough in savings to help cover the enormous costs of moving, and the unavoidable decrease in productivity that we suffered during the months following the quake," says Lamar. "It took us about six months to get the studio back up to speed, and even though we lost money during that time, our studio's financial situation never deteriorated to the point at which financial strain would have become another crushing blow to add to the damage that the earthquake had already caused. Because we were in solid financial shape, we didn't suffer nearly as much as some of the other businesses in our area did."

■ *Can I be sure that it won't become out-dated quickly?* Especially with computer equipment, this is a real concern. Look for a system that meets your current needs but can easily be expanded or inexpensively upgraded as both new technologies and your use of different capabilities grow.

■ *Are my current overhead costs manageable?* If you already have substantial overhead costs, then you must look for ways to cut overhead in other categories before taking on new financial burdens. If you really need the equipment, you may have to make trade-offs with your other costs.

■ *Is demand for my design work steady and growing?* While a new design system can help bring in new business, you should be building on a solid base of existing clients.

■ *Are there tax advantages for my studio if I own the equipment and apply the depreciation to my balance sheet?* For most businesses, there *are* such tax advantages, but make sure they help outweigh the costs of financing the purchase. Your accountant or attorney can advise you on this point.

■ *How much will training expenses add to the total cost?* This is an additional cost you may not have considered in figuring out whether your studio can afford the equipment. Leasing is often a safer option for a studio trying out new equipment. If the answer to any of the questions below is negative, you should probably play it safe and avoid a new long-term debt obligation by leasing the equipment instead of purchasing it.

■ *Am I sure that this is the right design system for me?* While almost every computer company in business now lets you try out its equipment before making any kind of commitment to buy or lease it, most companies offer two-week or thirty day trial periods; be sure you ask for one. Problems may arise down the road that couldn't be foreseen during your initial trial. For this reason, leasing may be a better option because repairs or upgrades can be handled by the lessor.

■ *Can the equipment be repaired easily or does it come with a warranty?* Some types of office machinery, such as copiers, need regular service and break down often. For these items, leasing may be better, since it puts the burden of maintenance on the equipment's owner, not you. Make sure your leasing contract stipulates that the lessor handles repairs.

■ *What happens if I just lease my equipment but find out that I really like it and want to keep it after the lease term is complete?* Many leases have a nominal buy-out clause. This gives you the benefits of a lease situation with the option to purchase the equipment after the leasing contract runs out.

■ *What happens if I find it's not the equipment I really need or want, or I run into financial difficulties?* It's a lot easier and financially much less risky to get out of a short-term lease than to sell a piece of used equipment, hoping the proceeds will be sufficient to pay off the original purchase loan.

CHAPTER ONE
TROUBLESHOOTERS

Q. *The overhead for my studio is fairly reasonable. It's the variable costs that are killing me! Some months when I look at the cash flow statement, we seem to be in good shape; other months we're barely scraping by because of high variable costs, like supplies and freelancers' wages. What should I do?*

A. First, average out your variable costs over the last nine months to see if you're really spending too much. If you had spent the *average* each month, would profitability have been acceptable? If not, reduce the monthly average by 10 to 20 percent, and then try to average less than that amount for the next few months. Are you handling projects on too short deadlines, thus requiring more staff per project? You might try to hire fewer freelancers, and ask your staff to pitch in and handle more work in-house. Just because certain costs are variable doesn't mean you can't control or reduce them when your studio needs to.

Q. *I will be applying for a bank loan soon to fund some expansions in my studio (additional staff and equipment). I know the loan officer will want to see a business plan for my studio, and I won't have any trouble coming up with the financial part of the plan (cash flow and income statements and projections). The problem is that I don't know what to say about my company's plans for the future, such as developing a timetable for expansion. I'd rather play it by ear. What should I say in my business plan?*

A. No one expects a business plan to be written in stone. But, it is a good idea to make some projections and plans for your studio's expansion, and put them in writing, if for no other reason than to keep track of your progress and remain clear and focused about your business and goals. A great deal will change as your business develops over the coming years, and it will help to have a written record of what you expected to compare with what really happens. Your business plan will also show how your short-term goals evolve to satisfy the long-term design goals you have. The narrative portion of the business plan is just as important as the financial section, and loan officers give equal weight to both. They want to see where the money is going, how it will help you succeed, and assure themselves that you can repay the loan.

Q. *A recent plumbing problem in the building damaged some flat files in my studio. Although the damage was covered by my insurance policy, I'm wondering about other equipment in the studio. What about coverage, for instance, if it was my telephone system or copier that was damaged, both of which I am currently leasing?*

A. You should check your leasing agreements immediately to make sure the equipment is covered. Always check any lease agreement before you sign it to find out if it contains insurance coverage, and if so, who pays for it. People often lease because they don't want to buy equipment—but if the equipment is damaged or destroyed *without insurance coverage*, lessees can end up "owning" (and making monthly payments on) worthless equipment.

CHAPTER ONE
CHECKLISTS

Use a business plan to:
- [ ] Focus your business and goals.
- [ ] Keep track of progress towards goals.
- [ ] Pinpoint potential pitfalls.
- [ ] Highlight potential growth areas.
- [ ] Explain your studio's financial plans to lending agents.

Include the following sections in your business plan:
- [ ] Mission statement.
- [ ] Executive summary.
- [ ] Table of contents.
- [ ] Business background.
- [ ] Short- and long-term business goals.
- [ ] Current goals.
- [ ] Situation analysis.
- [ ] Marketing strategy.
- [ ] Financial plans.
- [ ] Plan implementation time schedule.

While writing your business plan:
- [ ] Document your plan with supporting facts throughout, especially when commenting on market strategy, position and financial projections.

- [ ] Set ambitious but realistic financial goals.
- [ ] Work with your accountant to estimate projected income and expenses.
- [ ] Consider using a business plan software package to write your plan.

To cut costs and expenses:
- [ ] Keep lease commitments short-term.
- [ ] Keep salaried staff to a minimum.
- [ ] Invest in marketing, not equipment.
- [ ] Trim the excess.

Be sure to consider these workspace options:
- [ ] Home studios.
- [ ] Cooperative studios.
- [ ] Leasing studio space.
- [ ] Buying studio space.

When leasing studio space:
- [ ] Look for a creative, rather than corporate, atmosphere.
- [ ] Take into account the costs of renovation and their feasibility.
- [ ] Lease space that includes room for expansion.

☐ Create a separate space for client conferences or presentations.
☐ Create separate spaces for work that requires concentration or privacy.

It's best to acquire equipment when:
☐ Expected revenues will more than cover the associated costs.
☐ Equipment won't become outdated quickly.
☐ Your studio's current overhead and expenses *plus* the new acquisition costs are still manageable.
☐ Demand for your work is steady and sufficient.
☐ Tax advantages can help defray its impact on profits.
☐ You can afford the costs of training employees to use it.

Lease equipment instead of buying it if:
☐ You want to try out several different systems.
☐ Your long-term profitability is expected to be unstable.
☐ Your accountant or attorney recommends it for tax advantages.

CHAPTER 2

MAKING YOUR TIME COUNT

PROFIT POINTS

Practical strategies help you identify priorities, avoid distractions, and capitalize on good decisions by:

- Learning how to spend half the time on projects yet be twice as productive.
- Keeping control of multiple projects.
- Making sure top priorities don't get lost in the shuffle.
- Making your workspace more efficient.

In a design business, organizing your time well is particularly important because the product you are creating (your designs) demands a great deal of time for both creation and execution. Nothing looks worse or will damage your professional reputation more than hurriedly conceived and sloppily put together design. If you're trying to be creative when you are overbooked and overburdened, that strain can't help but result in poor quality design work. Your professional reputation and the business you bring in and retain depend on consistent, quality work. Simply stated, effective studio time management equals profits.

Designers who manage their time poorly frequently find themselves pushed into a corner and choose to let their businesses suffer rather than cut corners on their designs. But neglecting the practical end of your business can have equally devastating effects. If you don't keep a sharp eye on profits, costs, marketing and cash flow, you may not *have* a design business for long.

CONFRONTING PROCRASTINATION

If creating a company logo were the same as building a birdfeeder, it would be easy to figure out how much time each design would take. The problem is that while some designs come together naturally, others are a constant struggle, from the first sketches to the finished design. In a creative field like design, the natural question is: How can I manage my time when I never know how much of it I have and how much of it I'm going to need?

Another problem that people in all creative professions face is procrastination. It's not that procrastination is unique to artists, but that we often have a tougher time with it than people who work in less creative fields. Artists aren't lazy; the delay usually results from our subconscious fear of the eventual judgment of our work. Because we are artists, our egos are more tightly tied to our products than are those of people working in less creative fields. That makes it more difficult for us to fight the fear of judgment that sometimes results in procrastination.

Another reason effective time management is problematic for artists is that the work itself is so draining. Unless you are on a real creative streak, it is hard to work continuously on creative tasks for more than a few hours. Because so much of design work comes from within and is done without supervision, designers often end up as their own chief clockwatchers and critics—never an easy position in which to find oneself.

Balancing Creative and Regular Energy

The key to working efficiently in a creative profession is recognizing the ebb and flow of your own creative energy. Every designer is different, but almost invariably, each has particular periods of the day when ideas flow more naturally. For many people, this creative time is in the first few hours of the workday; for others the late afternoon or early evening is more productive. When you've pinpointed your high energy period you can isolate that time and use it to good advantage. Following are a few tips to help you do just that:

■ *Recognize your creative time.* Examine the way you divide tasks in a normal workday, and try to get a sense of when you find it easier to do design work rather than mundane chores. Make sure you block out that time each day strictly for using your creative energy and nothing else.

■ *Set aside hours to create.* Once you have blocked out your creative time, make it sacred. For instance, if you find your most productive hours are between 8:30 A.M. and 11 A.M., plan your work week as if you won't be in your office before eleven. Schedule meetings and business tasks around those prime hours. If at all possible, shut your office door and switch on your answering machine, or have the receptionist hold your calls. Leave tasks like open-

PERSONAL PROFILE

LYLE METZDORF
Lyle Metzdorf, Inc.
New York, New York

Lyle Metzdorf is a man who believes in setting goals and planning how to reach them. Fresh out of the Kansas City Art Institute & School of Design, he started as a mechanical paste-up man at a small ad agency and told himself then that at age thirty he would have his own agency. He did. He decided to sell that business by the time he was fifty. He did—at age forty-eight. Now Metzdorf is president of another business, the advertising and design firm Lyle Metzdorf, Inc., in New York City. And he's still setting goals and planning how to achieve them.

"Managing how you spend your workday is terribly important, because the time will be 'spent' whether or not you decide how to use it," says Metzdorf. He usually plans the week's work over the preceding weekend, and he keeps a daily logbook that schedules his time down to the quarter hour.

Metzdorf believes in closely scheduling his staff's time as well. He produces daily time sheets for each project his staff is handling. These sheets show who will do what toward the finished product on that particular day, and how much time each task is allotted. With such exact planning, Metzdorf, his staff, and his clients are always completely clear about how projects are progressing. Snags in the workflow are immediately apparent and consequently are more easily remedied.

"Using the daily time sheets, we can prepare a weekly status sheet to send to each client. And when we need an estimate for a new job, it is fairly easy to gauge the costs using the time sheets for a similar project as a model," Metzdorf notes.

ing the mail or returning phone calls until another time. Try to have all the supplies and equipment you will need on hand the night before, so you will be ready to roll when the time is right and your creative energies are percolating.

■ *Ask others to respect your time.* Spread the word about your "creative time." When you leave messages, make it clear that you cannot be reached before or after a certain time. Make a colorful "Do Not Disturb" sign for your door and ask co-workers to knock only as a last resort. You'll be amazed at how quickly creativity can become a conditioned response to a regular, quiet time set aside for it.

■ *Accept your creative rhythms.* Be attuned to the ebb and flow of your creativity. Some days you'll be able to design like a demon and will barely notice when your block of time is over. Other days, you'll be played out after an hour. The trick is to still keep that time for *creativity*. If you can't work on a particular design any further for the moment, start work on another project, or simply sketch and play around with general design ideas that have

nothing to do with projects you're working on now. When you are on a roll, try not to work past the point where you are truly into what you're doing. It's best to end on a high note, so you'll remember being inspired, not frustrated, or tapped out, when you sit down to work on the same project the next time.

TRIED AND TRUE TIME-SAVERS

Try keeping a log book for several weeks, charting exactly when you accomplish what you do. The patterns of time use the logbook reveals may surprise you. While learning accepted time management techniques can be helpful, the best ways to handle work efficiently can sometimes be those that you devise yourself to help you gain control over your time.

Time management is a personal issue; techniques should match your personal style. Don't try to use techniques that just aren't you—in the end you'll waste more time than you save and lose profits along the way. Techniques that feel more comfortable can help you achieve efficiency in your workday.

You'll have more success getting your time use under control if you combine several different techniques and styles, taking aspects from each that sound workable and reasonable to you. There are a myriad of books on the subject of time management, and efficiency consultants galore. Keep in mind: Time management advice is *only useful to the extent that you actually make use of it in your real, day-to-day life*. There are some great theories out there that would have your life run like a tight ship, but many don't leave time for the realities of life, like a sick child or an "off" day.

With that in mind, choose from the following time management techniques those that you feel can increase your efficiency while still suiting your temperament. If you have an idea that could make these techniques more useful for you, give that a try too.

■ *Keep a daily planner/diary.* Even if you're not the type that plots out the day in 15-minute increments, simple entries in a datebook can make scheduling projects easier. Most designers are juggling several projects at once (as well as the regular, necessary tasks of running a business). Mistakes caused by schedule mixups are a sure way to lose a client. *Bonus*: The more accurate and thorough your day-planner entries, the simpler it is to document business tax deductions for expenses such as client lunches, travel, etc. (See Chapter Five for further advice on how to document your tax deductions.)

■ *Use the last fifteen minutes or so of the workday to make a To Do Tomorrow list.* It is important to do this at the end of the day, when you are already focused on work and priorities and current tasks are fresh in your mind. If you put off making the list until first thing tomorrow morning, you must take time to refocus into your work mode, and you run the risk of being daunted even before you begin the new day. If the list is on top of your desk when you sit down to work in the morning, its clear statement of priorities will immediately bring your tasks and goals for the workday into focus.

■ *Set, and then regularly review, your priorities.* Your "to do" list should be prioritized, and you should review it at different points during the day to make sure the urgency of certain tasks hasn't shifted. But be careful not to lose sight of the larger picture. Don't set up all of your days so you accomplish only one little thing after another; you could end up neglecting the sorts of larger tasks that keep a design business growing (e.g., developing a self-promotion campaign, exploring new markets and applications for your designs).

■ *Define broad, strategic goals in terms of concrete actions.* In keeping track of the larger picture, you are bound to come up with certain tangible goals, such as "Build a better rapport with staff" or "Develop design colleague network." Forming such goals shows that you're looking toward the future growth of your business; however, it's easy to ignore such broad goals in favor of completing easy-to-handle tasks like "Order more paper" or "Send out week's invoices." To make strategic goals more manageable, break them down into specific actions. "Spend one hour during the coming week with each staff member to address his or her concerns," for example, is a concrete action for the less focused task of "Building better rapport with staff."

■ *Break larger projects into separate activities, and then those activities into manageable tasks.* For instance, instead of writing "Work on Chez Pierre menu design" on your To Do Tomorrow list, identify the part of the project on which you plan to work and then decide exactly what you want to accomplish: "Look at border designs for Chez Pierre menu and choose three options."

■ *Build "buffer" time into your schedule.* Most people find that it is easier to stick to a schedule if it allows leeway for unexpected interruptions and unforeseen complications. Many time management experts advise that only 60 percent of your time should be scheduled, and the other 40 percent should be used to accommodate overruns. Gauge how often such surprises are a problem for you, and build into your schedule the amount of time you think you need to handle them. This will help you avoid formulating a schedule that is too tight—or abandoning schedules all together because you find them unworkable.

■ *Never waste "down" time spent commuting or waiting for an appointment.* Use in-between time for reading industry journals, drafting letters, or even brainstorming about a new promotional mailing or design solution.

■ *Don't delay decisions and taking action.* This means responding to memos and letters on the first reading whenever possible, scheduling a lunch date or an appointment when it is first mentioned rather than saying, "Let's talk next week," and dictating a rough letter directly into a hand-held recorder while the letter's purpose is still fresh in your mind rather than just making a note to yourself to write the letter. Every once in a while you will have second thoughts, but it's better to go back and change a few decisions than to constantly postpone them and be forced to rethink problems from scratch each time they're called to your attention.

■ *Delegate, delegate, delegate.* For a small business entrepreneur, this is the hardest lesson to learn. Ask yourself: Are you still performing tasks for which you are far too qualified (or perhaps under qualified, such as accounting) simply because you can't bear to give up control and let someone else handle it? This is the quickest way to drive yourself crazy, and to drive your business into the ground.

■ *Arrange your workspace for maximum efficiency.* Make sure furniture, bookshelves, etc., are located so access is comfortable and workable. Keep often-used reference materials (such as your Rolodex, type books, color charts, telephone books, dictionary, thesaurus) in close proximity. Post a large wipe-off calendar on a wall within arm's reach of the telephone so project deadlines and appointments can be scheduled as they are made.

■ *Set an absolute deadline for little, bothersome tasks that never seem to get done.* Some chores, like straightening out a supply closet or sorting through unsolicited portfolios from illustrators, just never seem to get done

and *won't* get done unless you purposely set aside the time on your list to do them. If a task hangs on your to-do list for more than a week, ask yourself: "Can I drop it from the list? Set aside a time to handle it? Pass it on to someone else?" Choose one of these three options, and then be done with it.

■ *Know when to stop.* Perfectionism usually costs more than it is worth. Ask yourself which tasks deserve the extra effort required to make them absolutely perfect and which tasks are fine if just done well. The slight difference between "well done" and "perfect" is rarely noticed by others, but can cost your business plenty in time and energy.

THE ENEMY

Two of the biggest enemies known to time management are the telephone and the meeting. These two activities are time consuming for any businessperson, but when you're trying to run your own business they can be even bigger problems because you're trying to be all things to all people—your clients, your staff and yourself.

It's easy to simply tell yourself to spend less time on the telephone or to focus your meetings so they move along more quickly. But that is not enough. To really work more efficiently, you must retrain yourself to limit time spent in both areas and to make sure that the time you do spend is well spent. Here are some guidelines:

The Telephone

■ When receiving calls, be clear about how much time you have. If the call is not vital, don't hesitate to say, "I'm in the middle of something, but I have a minute. What can I do for you?"

■ When you're making calls and time is tight, try to limit your conversation to efficiently, yet cordially, taking care of your business. Try calling with: "Hi, Mr. Evans, this is Jan Schmidt. Do you have a moment to answer a question about the sketches you sent me last Tuesday?" The busy person you're calling will appreciate your getting to the point.

■ Make a list of topics to cover before you make a call. This will help you organize your thinking, and possibly save you the bother of having to make an extra call to add something you forgot. Having a list in front of you can help calm "telephone jitters," especially if a difficult client is on the line or you're calling someone you don't know.

■ To end a call, say, "Sounds like we've covered everything. I'll let you get back to work." If a caller doesn't get the hint, say something like "We'll have to discuss this further at another time. Right now, I have to get to a meeting (answer a call on another line, etc.)."

Meetings

■ Make sure a meeting is necessary before you call or agree to one. Can you relay the same information in a quick memo, or even by letting the right people know when you meet them at the coffee machine? Can you ask the person to send you a proposal in written form rather than requiring you to attend a meeting?

■ Never meet without an agenda. Compose the agenda, and send it to meeting participants beforehand. That way, people can bring any pertinent information they'll need to discuss the topics planned, rather than offering the perpetual "I'll have to get back to you on that; the figures aren't in front of me." An agenda also helps keep meetings focused rather than allowing people to stray off on tangents.

■ Limit the number of meeting attendees to no more than ten if decisions are to be reached during that meeting. It is easier for a smaller group to make decisions than it is for a larger one. Unproductive meetings don't just waste your time, they also waste your business's money: 1 hour-long useless meeting × 8 staff members = 1 billable workday lost (8 hours).

■ End each meeting by asking one participant to fill out an "action sheet" instead of keeping minutes. An action sheet has spaces in which to list date, time, meeting partici-

pants, actions agreed upon, who will handle each action, and what the deadline for each action is. A copy of the action sheet should be sent to each meeting participant, so you can all keep up with each other's progress.

HOW TO MANAGE MULTIPLE PROJECTS

One planning skill that is crucial to design studios is project management. Whether designing a simple print ad or creating a whole new corporate identity and ad campaign, a designer's work usually breaks down into *projects* that are made up of smaller individual tasks. Your job as a business owner/designer/project manager is to coordinate all of these smaller tasks and the people who do them so the project gets done in the most efficient way possible. Efficiency in project management means two things for a designer: more creative and beautifully executed designs *and* more profits.

Planning a new project will become easier as you gain more experience in project management. The first few times you set up a project schedule, you may find that you have underestimated the time needed for certain tasks while leaving far too many hours for others. You will invariably overlook at least one big pitfall that will throw the whole project into crisis, at least for a few hours. But as you learn from your mistakes, your project planning will become more exact and more useful.

Besides averting the emotional turmoil that unforeseen problems create, a project plan (a written schedule of when each phase of the project will be completed, and by whom) can also help reassure your client of exactly what she will be getting for her money. A sensible, matter-of-fact project plan can help convince clients who don't really understand what a designer does or how he does it that they will be getting their money's worth.

Deadlines

There is one golden rule of project management: Never, ever, set a final deadline that you will not be able to keep. A client may be making all kinds of plans that incorporate your design, and if you cannot deliver the work on time, the consequences may be serious. Missing an important deadline is probably the most unprofessional thing a designer can do. Don't fall into the trap of agreeing to an early deadline that you're not sure you can meet because the client is pressuring you to hurry. The lasting evidence of your work for a client is the design itself, not how quickly you did it, and you want the design to be the best it can be, not the fastest it can be. Take the time you need to do the job well.

Formulating a Project Plan

Following are some guidelines that will help you formulate an effective, reasonable project plan:

■ *Know thyself.* Before you can make a realistic estimate of how long any one task will take, you must appraise your staff's workstyles, skills and talents. The mistake that most beginning project managers make is being too ambitious. Try to look at the tasks with optimism, but also frankness: Can the person really work productively eleven hours a day, or is it more like seven? Are you and your staff well organized? How long are creative energy spans? Are you and your staff easily distracted or discouraged? You will be doing no one a favor by ignoring the less-than-desirable aspects of people's work styles in formulating your project plan.

■ *Recognize that priorities change.* Unless your studio is underworked, you will usually have at least two projects going at once, and there may be a need to shift schedules as each one vies for attention.

■ *Set daily goals/deadlines.* This is one way to keep close tabs on how well you are progressing toward the finished product. Reaching a daily goal gives encouragement and a small sense of accomplishment. Use this as a cross-check with your daily to-do list.

■ *Schedule around—don't put off—regular commitments.* If you put everything on hold to concentrate only on the project at hand, you'll wind up bored with working constantly on one

thing. And besides that, everything that you postponed will suddenly loom like a mountain before you when the final deadline is met. Instead of being able to savor the elation of completing a project, you will feel daunted and discouraged.

■ *Establish a deadline that includes plenty of time for contingencies.* After you've built time into the project schedule to cover things that could go wrong, expand the schedule to include time to handle the things you haven't even thought of. The key to setting a project deadline is to make sure you can meet it. Period. Take an example from the airlines: Fliers used to complain that flights always arrived late. The airlines started adding contingency time—for weather, crowded runways, and other unforeseeable problems—to their estimated times of arrival. Suddenly flights were almost always on time, or even early. Flight durations had not changed one bit—but fliers were happy now that the arrival times they had been promised were being met.

■ *Involve the entire project team when you are planning a project.* Besides getting your staff's estimates of the time it takes *them* to complete their own tasks, there are two other important contributions they can make: Team members can give information and advice about issues or problems you might not have considered. And secondly, everyone on staff is more likely to cooperate if they're included in the project's planning stages. By including paste-up people and support staff in the planning, you make the design project *theirs,* and people will always work harder and more carefully on something they have a stake in.

■ *List and define all the different project tasks explicitly, and draw connections between them.* Since designers are visually oriented, present them with a chart showing the tasks and the connections between them. This graphic illustration of the work at hand makes it easier for everyone to understand their part in the project. By drawing connections between tasks, you are also showing people how the quality of their work and their ability to meet internal deadlines affects the work of other team members. It's harder to slouch when the potential consequences of slacking off are right there in black and white.

Project Management Options

Depending on the size of your staff and the temperament of your studio, projects can be managed in one of two ways:

Traditional style. You choose the people best suited for each task, and let them loose. For a small project or small staff, this method may work well, but be aware that a leadership void can slow communication between project team members or create power struggles between individuals. Such difficulties will create down time and cause delays throughout the process, ultimately biting into profits.

Project structure. If you have a staff that includes several designers experienced enough to oversee a project by themselves, meet with project team members during the planning stage, then let the designer/project manager handle all subsequent questions and problems from team members. Involve yourself only as an overseer of the project as a whole. *Don't* make someone the project manager and then constantly interfere with the everyday workings of the project—you'll just end up frustrating project team members, the project manager, and yourself.

Software assistance

There are many fine project management software programs available that offer a multitude of benefits. Such programs can calculate efficiency factors into time required for tasks in hours and percentages of days, create GANTT charts that will break your project down into steps showing deadlines and work accomplished per task, and create network charts that show interdependencies of tasks. These programs also have the option of plan modification. When unforeseen tasks are added to the project midstream, you just add the tasks and hours required and all other charts, figures and plans are automatically adjusted. Some of these programs are: Microsoft Project, MacProject II, Time Line, Harvard Project

Manager, Project Workbench, and SYZYGY. They also allow you to print out daily and weekly project reports, estimate time needed and costs for each project with different sets of variables, and compute estimates and budgets quickly. Using such programs can be a major time-saver (and, thus, money saver) if you do the same types of design jobs regularly.

HELPING YOUR STAFF MANAGE THEIR TIME

Although you might feel you've gotten your work time use down to a science, your staff may not be in the same disciplined shape. You cannot remake each staff member in your own efficient image; you can (and should) help them use their work time more productively. A loss in staff productivity relates directly to a loss in profits, missed deadlines, and dissatisfied (and potentially lost) clients.

Before you begin your efficiency crusade, remember: Everyone is an individual; everyone has a different way of thinking about time and how to use it. While there are certain standards of efficiency needed to keep a business running well, it is not necessary that people do things exactly as you would. Your way is not necessarily the right way—it's the way that works best *for you.* In talking to your staff about how they use their time, keep varying work styles in mind and make respectful suggestions. This approach will meet with more cooperation than a blind insistence that all your people adopt the same strategies you use.

Employee Work Styles

The following list was compiled with the help of Sunny Schlenger, a personal management consultant and author of *How to Be Organized in Spite of Yourself,* Dutton, $4.95, to help you encourage productive time management in the various types of people you have working for you:

■ *Mr. Indecisive/Slow Start.* This is the individual who is generally overwhelmed at the enormity of the whole project, losing sight of individual tasks that should be accomplished one at a time, in succession. For this individual it is important to set up a time line for each project, breaking down the project into manageable tasks and including a date by which key decisions will have to be made. Make sure he knows what information and whose approval is needed in order to make a judgment call and move ahead. Show your faith in his ability to handle things well, giving encouragement when you can.

■ *Ms. Hopper.* This person flits from one task to the next, leaving all of them incomplete. She is easily bored and looks for things to get involved in. For this person, it is important to limit the number of projects she must juggle at once, but do not make her focus exclusively on one because she will quickly become bored and her work will suffer. If possible, design a work space for her that is free of distractions such as multiple phone lines that ring even if the call is for someone else. An office with a door that can be shut is also helpful.

■ *Mr. Thrive-on-Chaos.* This person claims the works best under pressure. He'll delay tasks until the last minute and create an atmosphere of panic and turmoil in your studio. It is important that you make his deadlines ironclad: "If this mechanical can't go to the printer by noon on August 3, we're dead." Ask him to let you know as soon as possible if a deadline looks unreachable. Try not to get caught up in, or be annoyed by, his last-minute frenzy, as long as his work is done well and on time.

■ *Ms. Perfection.* This is the typical, self-critical person who doesn't know when enough is enough. Make sure that she isn't putting too much effort into achieving perfection. Check periodically that she is clear on which work deserves priority status, watching also that she doesn't work too much overtime and get burned out.

■ *Mr. Allergic-to-Detail.* This person focuses on only the general concepts of the project, leaving details to an invisible "someone

PERSONAL PROFILE

KAREN SINGER
Designer
Philadelphia, Pennsylvania

"One thing art school doesn't prepare you for is success," observes Karen Singer, a Philadelphia designer and sculptor who specializes in architectural ceramics. "When my business began to take off during the last year or so, I was completely unprepared to handle the business end of my success. And the chief way in which my bewilderment showed itself was in my disorganized office space. Even the term 'office space' is a joke—my 'office' was numerous piles of paper stacked on the dining room table."

Singer's studio is in a separate building from her home office space, and she had no trouble keeping her design space organized and clear. But the office part of her business (in her home) was a mess. So she called in Sunny Schlenger, a personal management consultant and the president of Schlenger

Organizational Systems.

Schlenger decided that Singer was an "Everything Out" and a "Hopper," two personality types that she often finds among creative people. (See pages 21-23 for more on personality types.) An "Everything Out" likes to keep all papers in sight, albeit in organized piles, and a "Hopper" is someone who enjoys juggling several projects at once rather than following one from beginning to end and then moving on to the next.

"She helped me to sort through my mountains of paper and put them into three baskets: To Do, To File, and To Throw Away. She suggested I buy a rolling file cart to keep papers handy, and put a larger filing cabinet in the basement for long-term storage of files I'll only need occasionally. Then she helped me choose a desk with lots of surface area to set up expanding files for the several projects I have going at once. It's not so much that I had trouble being organized, it's that Sunny helped me to keep the information I need in a much more accessible way," says Singer.

else" to do. Work with him to plan a step-by-step schedule for projects rather than forcing a regimented plan on him. Suggest that he keep an expandable file on each project and review it regularly to make sure that details are being attended to. If possible, provide him with a support person (preferably a Ms. Perfectionist) to help him keep track of details.

HOW TO MAKE YOUR WORKSPACE MORE EFFICIENT

Throughout this chapter, we've discussed how time lost from inefficient work habits is equal to a loss in profits. There is an additional hidden source of wasted time that most people don't pay too much attention to, but should: An inefficiently designed workspace. How many times have you spent fifteen minutes or more hunting for a misplaced typebook or re-writing a letter because the original is nowhere to be found? If you are disorganized and want to get your office and design space in order, your first impulse may be to file everything neatly away. But efficient use of space is like productive use of time: Finding a system compatible with your own personal style is the key.

For instance, a new set of filing cabinets complete with an intricate filing system may set your affairs in order initially, but if your natural impulse is to keep all of your papers out in the open in neat (but unfiled) piles, your new filing drawers will stand empty while you continue to organize your same little piles on top of your desk. Instead of the inappropriate, intricate filing system, try a rolling, open file cart that can organize your papers yet still keep them within arm's reach. Make constructive use of your wall space: Buy a bulletin board, a wall-mounted plastic wipe-off calendar, and a set of slanted tier racks or wall pockets to hold current reference materials, reading matter, and correspondence.

While it is important to consider your personal style when trying to use space more efficiently, there are two basic principles that will help you keep your workspace workable no matter what your style:

■ *Make sure your workspace is comfortable and functional.* Such things as good lighting, well-designed furniture at the right angle and height, and a shaded computer screen to cut down on eye fatigue all count toward productivity.

■ *If possible, divide your workspace into two areas—a design area and an office area.* Your design space should include your drawing table, all design materials and equipment, and reference books specifically for design, such as type books. Lighting should be strong and easily adjustable. In your office space should be a desk, your telephone and computer, Rolodex, files, and bookkeeping ledgers. Besides the convenience of separating your two business functions, having two different areas will also help you to concentrate on the task at hand and keep you from being distracted by chores from the other side of the business.

CHAPTER TWO
TROUBLESHOOTERS

Q. *Every few months I make a resolution to schedule my time more efficiently. All goes well for the first few days, and then a crisis hits and my well-laid plans are blown to pieces. So why bother to schedule at all?*

A. Your problem may be that your schedules are too rigid for you to follow realistically. Are you building in enough contingency time? Are you estimating your efficiency at 100 percent or a more realistic 70 percent? In project planning, try to build in extra time to handle the unexpected, and keep your scheduling as flexible as possible within the bounds of effectiveness. Also, make sure you are not subconsciously sabotaging your schedules simply because you feel you *should* use formal schedules but resist using them to prove they don't work. Make a schedule you *can* live with, even if it is more liberal than the ideals that most time-management specialists recommend.

Q. *I am a pack rat. I simply cannot bear to throw anything out for fear that I may toss out something I'll need at a later date, like a letter or sketch. As a result, I end up sifting through the same heaps of paper over and over again. What should I do?*

A. When you receive a piece of paper, decide right then to act on it, pass it on, file it, or toss it. It helps to have a basket for each option. For items that don't belong to specific clients or projects, establish several new files: Good Sketches for Review, Product Literature, and a General File for future reference. You'll make a set of these three files each month. At the end of the month, toss the unused contents of the set that is at least six months old.

Q. *I know that there is a growing need in my studio for regular project status meetings, but we're so busy and employees are already stretched so thin. What can I do?*

A. Meetings can be time wasters or time-savers, depending on your approach. Especially in a busy studio, regularly scheduled staff/ project status meetings with a time limit—say every Tuesday morning from 8:30 A.M. to 9:30 A.M.—will be effective for a number of reasons. These meetings will be regular forums for problem solving, eliminating some of the normal interruptions that waste time. They will also provide an opportunity for open communication in your studio. Since projects will be discussed, all employees will know what everyone else is doing.

CHAPTER TWO
CHECKLISTS

To make the best use of your creative energy's ebb and flow:
- ☐ Determine your hours of peak creative energy.
- ☐ Block out creative time and make it sacred.
- ☐ Assemble materials beforehand.
- ☐ Limit interruptions during your peak hours.

Some tried and true ways to save time are to:
- ☐ Keep a daily planner.
- ☐ Write an end-of-the-day To Do Tomorrow list.
- ☐ Set priorities and periodically review them.
- ☐ Turn vague, intangible goals into smaller, concrete tasks.
- ☐ Divide large projects into smaller, manageable tasks.
- ☐ Build buffer time into all schedules.
- ☐ Don't waste "down" time.
- ☐ Delegate smaller decisions on the spot.
- ☐ Organize your work space efficiently.
- ☐ Set absolute deadlines for easy-to-put-off tasks.
- ☐ Make something *perfect* only when it needs to be.

To keep meetings time-efficient:
- ☐ Only meet when absolutely necessary.
- ☐ Always set an agenda.
- ☐ Limit the number of attendees.
- ☐ Keep action sheets instead of minutes.

To make each telephone call count:
- ☐ Be clear about how much time you have to talk.
- ☐ Make a list of topics to cover.

- ☐ End too-long conversations pleasantly but firmly.

Project Management:
- ☐ Know your own work pace and time-use patterns.
- ☐ Understand that changing priorities can cause delays.
- ☐ Set frequent internal deadlines and goals.
- ☐ Schedule around regular commitments.
- ☐ Factor in time for contingencies.
- ☐ Encourage all team members to share their concerns when setting a project schedule.
- ☐ Detail each step of each project task.
- ☐ Draw connections between related tasks.

Help your staff manage their time productively by:
- ☐ Recognizing that your way is not the *only* right way to allot time.
- ☐ Using the approach best suited to each staff member.
- ☐ Playing on their strengths.
- ☐ Avoiding or backing up each person's weak areas.

Make the best use of your space by:
- ☐ Making sure your workspace is both comfortable and functional—have adequate lighting, well-defined and suitable furniture, and keep reference materials within arm's reach.
- ☐ Dividing workspace into two separate areas for design work and administrative work.

CHAPTER 3
GETTING PAID . . . WELL AND ON TIME

PROFIT POINTS

Price your jobs profitably and get paid on time by:

- Knowing how to set (and raise) standard job rates.
- Getting what you want during negotiation.
- Keeping the usage rights you need to reap future financial benefits.
- Bringing in money faster while retaining your clients' good will.
- Stressing the benefits of immediate payment.
- Dealing with clients who don't pay.

Over the last few years, as our society's communication has become increasingly visual, design has become more highly valued. As savvy businesspeople, designers must realize that their talents are more in demand and more highly prized than ever before. Accordingly, they must learn to value their skills and price jobs in relation to their experience, talent and expertise, in addition to figuring in things like what the competition charges, research, and usage and circulation of the design.

This chapter will help you figure out how to price jobs profitably, charge for expense overruns and revisions, deal with vendors, and how to bill and collect fees. Another excellent source of information for pricing jobs is the Graphic Artists Guild's *Pricing and Ethical Guidelines*, distributed by North Light Books. No designer's reference bookshelf is complete without it.

SETTING JOB RATES

Hourly Rates

The basic building block used to price most jobs is the hourly rate. The hourly rate is partially based on what your per-hour expenses are, making it easier to price jobs knowing that a profit is built into the rate. Unless your studio is a one-person company, you might want to calculate two separate hourly rates, one for your time or other partner or principal designer's time, and one for your employees' time. The two rates are calculated differently because an hour of design time is worth much more than an hour of paste-up or clerical time, and, accordingly, the client should pay more for design time.

To calculate an hourly rate for your time, add together all of your studio's annual overhead costs. Use last year's numbers unless you've just opened your studio or your expenses this year are radically different from last year's. If you've been in operation less than a year, figure out your average monthly expenses and multiply them by twelve. Be sure to include overhead costs here, such as rent or mortgage, employee benefits, non-reimbursable office and art supplies, equipment depreciation, taxes, a client entertainment or presentation budget, promotion costs, legal and financial advice, utilities, insurance, and employees' salaries plus your own.

Once you have the annual total, divide the number by 1,000 hours per year. A fifty-week, thirty-five hour a week schedule would have you working a total of 1,750 hours a year, but at least 750 of those hours are spent handling the tasks of running a studio that are not billable to any one client—promotion and marketing, client presentations, writing job proposals, hiring and managing staff. So for this reason, you divide the annual overhead expenses by only your billable hours (around 1,000) for the year. For instance, if total overhead is $130,000 (including your salary), then 130,000 divided by 1,000 = 130 or $130 per hour. This hourly rate covers the hourly cost of running your studio and your design time.

To calculate an hourly rate for employees, the formula is slightly different. Since you have already calculated studio overhead into your (or the designer's) hourly rate, you should simply take the employee's annual salary and divide it by 1,500 hours. The reason the total is divided by 1,500 for employees is because, unlike a design principal/entrepreneur, they spend most of their hours at work doing tasks that *are* billable to a client. For instance, if you pay a production artist $40,000 a year, his or her annual salary divided by 1,500 hours is 40,000 divided by 1,500 = 26.66, or around $27 an hour.

Using these hourly rates, you can make a rough estimate of whether or not a job will be profitable for you at a certain price. For example, if a client offers you $3,000 for a job that you estimate will take 15 employee hours at

PERSONAL PROFILE

LORI SEIBERT
Seibert Design Associates, Inc.
Cincinnati, Ohio

Few designers have come as far as fast as Lori Seibert. She left *Visual Merchandising & Store Design* magazine in 1987 to open her own studio as a sole proprietor with a single assistant. Four years later, she heads up a team of four graphic designers, and her studio is an incorporated business called Seibert Design Associates, Inc. That's a long way in four short years!

The designers at Seibert Design Associates each follow their own projects from conception through mechanicals, and each has their own clients with whom they do business. Instead of segmenting the job functions at SDA into client rep, designer, and production positions, Seibert prefers to let designers develop and track projects in their entirety, although designers sometimes do trade off tasks according to who is overloaded and who has free time. She, and clients such as Formica, National Cash Register, Beckett Paper, and Mercy Health Systems, find that this "jack-of-all-trades" approach to graphic design can work beautifully.

Seibert has a novel approach to pricing jobs: She asks clients for their opinions. Seibert explains, "With clients I know well and trust, I will often ask how my bid looks in comparison to other bidders'. I know this behavior may sound naive, and I wouldn't do this with just anyone, but I have actually had clients tell me that they felt I was pricing myself under my worth in the current market. Because in design your colleagues are also your competitors, it can be hard to 'ask around' for pricing advice. Who is in a better position than a client you know and trust to give you a solid idea of how your prices compare?"

Seibert also uses comparable past jobs to come up with an initial, ballpark figure. "I find that non-labor costs are usually fairly easy to estimate if you have a basic idea of the kind of design that will work well for a particular project," she says. "For instance, a simple, two-color job is, of course, going to cost a lot less in supplies and printing than an intricate, eight-color extravaganza. But past jobs can be useful in calculating the labor required to put together a certain type of

design. One of the greatest learning tools around is to make a large miscalculation in the hours a certain job is going to take. When you look at that job file and see how many extra, unbudgeted, unpaid hours you put in, it's harder to make the same mistake again.

"I also find it helpful to ask a client in the first meeting what kind of budget he or she has in mind for the project," Seibert continues. "This serves two purposes. First, it helps me keep in mind what kind of design I should plan for a client, so that I don't spend time and energy cooking up a 'champagne' design for someone with a 'beer' budget. Secondly, it keeps me from putting my time into a well-thought-out proposal and then finding out that the client was planning on spending an amount that could barely cover my overhead. It just helps to know whether you and the client are even in the same neighborhood, pricewise."

Another pricing practice that has worked well for Seibert is not only estimating hourly labor costs, but breaking them down by the kind of labor and the associated hourly charge. For instance, she may divide a design project into time for research, design, refinement, production, and photo art direction or press supervision, and charge different hourly rates for each of those functions, even if the same designer is covering all of them. She feels that pricing a job this way helps a client to understand how much each different stage of the design job costs in labor, and how she gets to the total fee. She also finds that clients really like knowing, as minutely as possible, exactly where their money is going, and that solid, work-hour figures help to reassure them.

"The general feedback I've gotten from clients is that our prices are at the high end of the middle range, and that's exactly where I want Seibert Design Associates to be. Although I have taken design jobs at a discounted price because I hoped to develop a relationship and eventually do more work for the same client, in general I think that 'lowballing' or price cutting hurts the graphic design industry and gives a designer a reputation as 'cheap'. Companies do ask each other about the 'going rate' for design jobs," Seibert notes, "and if your studio is often mentioned as the least expensive, it will be tough on your business when you eventually raise your prices to a level that reflects your talent."

$27 each and 25 design hours at $130 each, the $3,000 will not even cover your hourly rate total: (15 × $27) + (25 × $130) = $3,655. You must either scale down the job, get more money from the client, or take a loss. It is also important to consider any special new expenses that are unique to the project you are being asked to design, for example the rent of special pieces of video equipment.

Hourly rates vary a great deal depending on what kind of design you do and what area of the country you work in. For up-to-date figures on typical hourly and job rates, consult the most recent edition of the *Pricing and Ethical Guidelines*.

Standard Rates

If you do many jobs that are similar, you may also want to set a standard job rate, say, for jobs like sixty-four-page annual reports or two-color, type-only letterheads. Never quote these standard rates to a client. Use them for your own purposes as a starting point for figuring out what to charge. No matter how similar, each job has its own character and potential pitfalls, and you must make sure you value your own work fairly. Don't stick to a total just because it's your standard rate.

For setting standard job rates, it is very important that your records of past jobs be complete and accurate. If you don't keep thorough time sheets, for instance, it is difficult to estimate how long a certain job may take you the next time you have a similar one. Accurate job files can help insure that you end up pricing jobs profitably. After all, if you don't estimate accurately, you might not make the profit you could have if you had referred to your old job sheets.

Page Rates

Some designers price print work as a percentage of the advertising page rate of the publication in which the work appears. For instance, if a designer does a color cover for a magazine with a page rate of $50,000, the charge is $50,000 × .15 = $7,500. Since ad page rates for magazines are largely dependent on the magazine's circulation, this type of pricing takes into account how many people will see your design. There are different percentages charged for black-and-white and color pages and spreads, and for editorial or advertising use, ranging from 10 percent to 17.5 percent.

PRICING JOBS MORE PROFITABLY

Take heart: Pricing jobs gets easier with experience. But to eliminate at least some of the guesswork, the following section outlines three methods for pricing a job. It may be a good idea to use each method on the same job in order to come up with rough numbers, and then to reconcile and refine the total toward the price that you think is most fair and accurate.

The Overhead/Hourly-Rate Method

Some designers simply gauge how many hours a job will take, total the hourly rate (using the overhead formula above), increase that total by 50 percent to 100 percent, and add on a pretax profit percentage (10 percent to 25 percent, depending on factors such as your studio's reputation and the current health of the design industry). For instance, if you estimate that a job will take thirty hours of your time (at $95 an hour), and forty hours of employee time (at $28 an hour), add those two totals (30 × 95 = 2850; 40 × 28 = 1120; 2850 + 1120 = $3,970). Then add on 75 percent more to cover expenses such as supplies, messengers, and typography. Finally, add on your typical profit margin, and you'll end up with a rough idea of what the client should pay for the job, including expenses ($3,970 × 1.75 = $6,947.50 + [$6,947.50 × 0.17 ÷ by (1 - 0.17)] = $8,370.48). Using detailed time sheets like the one shown on page 30 will provide great help in keeping and charging for time appropriately.

The Market Rate Method

Although less precise, this way of estimating prices can be helpful. Simply use all of your resources to calculate what the recent rate has been for similar jobs. Consult your old job files, ask other designers or art directors, check published pricing guidelines, and even check competitor quotes with the client himself. By balancing out the different numbers you get from checking around, you'll gain a sense of what the going price is.

The Itemized Pricing Method

Itemizing costs is something you will have to do anyway when you draw up a contract and bill for the job, but doing it during the pricing stage can help you come up with a more accurate bid. Basically, you just add together all of the costs involved in the job (expenses + labor + profit) for a price total.

Beyond the costs of materials and other expenses and labor, there are other points to consider when pricing a job. For instance, will four hundred people see the design or four hundred million? Will it be reproduced for a limited time, or does it become the property of the client, like a logo. Other factors that can't

necessarily be measured in dollars and cents but that you should take into account when pricing a job are listed below:

■ *Usage rights.* This is probably the single most important point to consider in selling a design. The more rights to a design the client wants to buy, the higher the price for the design should be. For some designs, you might sell only one-time usage rights, while for others (like a corporate logo), a buyer should acquire all or most of the rights to the design. (See the discussion on contracts and rights later in this chapter.) If, after you've completed a design, a client wants additional usage rights, you should charge extra for them.

■ *Licensing and royalties.* If your client plans on marketing an item using your design, you may miss out on potential licensing and

FOR FREELANCERS:

T I M E   S H E E T

address _____

phone number _____

social security number _____

signature _____

approval signature _____

hours worked _____

hourly rate _____

total _____

Please turn in original and one copy to us, and keep one copy for yourself.

Corey McPherson Nash

name _____

day & date _____

job number	task number	hours

201. Client Meetings
202. In House Meetings
203. Supervision
204. Ideas
205. Design
206. Comprehensives
207. Layouts
208. Type Specifications
209. Mechanical Preparation
210. Color Preparation
211. Copywriting
212. Illustration
213. Photo Art Direction
214. Review of Proofs
215. Press Run
216. Writing Specs
217. Travel Time
218. Video Production
219. Research
220. Job Administration
221. Mac Typesetting
222. Other:
230. New Business
231. Office Adminstration
232. C&C:D Non Billable

★ To indicate AA's prefix these numbers with a 3.
ie: 209 = Mechanicals
309 = Mechanical AA's

Beth Maynard of Corey & Co. Designers uses this time sheet for three purposes. Staff designers use it as a daily record of time spent on design work and administrative (nonbillable) duties. The administrative staff uses it to record their activities for a week. Freelancers use it as an invoice. It has been used for over seven years because it so efficiently logs time to price jobs.

PERSONAL PROFILE

PAUL BASISTA
Graphic Artists Guild
New York, New York

"Pricing jobs profitably and being paid well for their work has always been tough for designers," says Paul Basista. Basista should know. He is executive director of the Graphic Artists Guild, a professional association dedicated to establishing fair and equitable industry practices. The Guild is located in New York City and has over 3,500 members. It produces a book many designers consider their bible — the Graphic Artists Guild's *Pricing and Ethical Guidelines*, a comprehensive outline of fair business practice, copyright law, pricing guidelines, and real dollar figures for fees in various areas of design. The book contains information about the business end of design that designers find invaluable.

Basista explains the difficulty in pricing design jobs: Designers usually do the bulk of their work in coming up with the design idea. Although executing the design takes time and a great deal of creativity, the idea itself is what gives a design most of its worth. Knowing how much time and effort must go into coming up with the right design idea is difficult. Because this can be hard to gauge, designers tend to underprice the idea-generating component of their work. Basista stresses the research that goes into creating the right design, especially for something like a company logo. "To create the right image," he says, "a designer may have to spend months learning about a company. He or she may end up interviewing its entire board of directors and even its employees and customers in the course of the research. The designer must understand how the company sees itself, what its present position is in its industry, the market position it is shooting for, and the nuances of how it would like to be perceived by its customers. These sometimes hard-to-pindown emotions, thoughts and perceptions must be translated into ink colors, shapes and typography. The ability to do that effectively is extremely valuable, but since part of creating a design involves using intuition and experience (both are hard to quantify), the development part of design work can be difficult to put a price tag on."

He continues, "We live in a society that is becoming increasingly visual. People don't stop to read the fine print anymore. The quick communication through visual images of all kinds of feelings and values is what is most effective today. And that is why the role of a designer has become more important than ever before. When you see a pair of yellow arches, you think 'McDonald's,' or a yellow parallelogram, you think 'Hertz'. The value of such universally understood design to a company's business is almost incalculable. Someone once said, 'Good design is good business,' and in our society, 'good business' translates directly into dollars. The designer who creates a design that helps generate business should get his or her full share of the dollars produced by the business."

Although Basista stresses that designers should price jobs according to their skills and talents, he points out that, a price estimate is often just a starting point in price negotiations. If a designer suspects that a client undervalues her skills and is thus trying to bargain down the price, she may take any haggling as a personal affront or devaluation of her work. Basista feels that this is not necessarily the right attitude. He says, "Negotiating is a part of doing business, even when the deal is over something as personal as artwork. If a client doesn't accept your initial price estimate, consider carefully whether you can do the job for less. For instance, can you get a better printing deal, do the job for slightly less because the exposure is valuable to you, agree to more restricted usage of the design, or take a smaller profit on this first job in order to develop the company as a steady client? While you don't want to cut below overhead costs and a decent salary for yourself and your employees, don't automatically reject a smaller fee without first considering whether you can still make the job worthwhile at the lower rate. Businesspeople are used to dickering over prices."

Basista warns that even once a price has been agreed upon by both the client and the designer, the fee negotiation isn't always over. "The Guild advises that a designer always add a revision or 'author's alterations' clause to the contract. If a client wants changes made *after* preliminary sketches have already been approved, then that extra design work must be billed as such. Rethinking a design takes a great deal of creative energy and maybe even additional research, and that is something you should *not* provide for the client at no extra charge."

royalty fees by charging a one-time, flat fee for your work. Consult an attorney with licensing and royalty experience before selling anything but one-time usage of a design. (Later in this chapter we'll discuss contracts and more detailed information on licensing and royalties.)

■ *Complexity.* If a design requires a great deal of research or an intricate production process, make sure the price reflects the extra work involved.

■ *Steady work or larger projects.* If a client asks you to design, say, a weekly, in-house newsletter, your per-job price may be slightly lower than if it were a one-shot deal, simply because a familiar job takes less time and creative effort than a completely new one. In situations such as these, make sure you get at least a short-term, say three-month, commitment from the client.

■ *Short deadlines.* If you must do a job quickly, you'll probably work overtime hours (e.g., weekends or evenings), and you may have to pay rush rates for outside services, such as stats or typography. Your price should reflect these extra costs.

■ *Circulation.* The more people that will look over your design work, the higher your fee should be.

■ *Consultations.* If you must meet more often than normal with an art director or client, figure that time (plus travel costs, if applicable) into your total fee.

■ *Taxes.* Don't forget to include state sales tax, if applicable.

■ *Vendors' services mark-up.* It is common practice to add around 20 percent to all vendors' prices on your itemized invoice to the client. This mark-up covers your costs of choosing the right vendor, overseeing his work, and the reduction in cash flow that results from paying the vendor's charges through your studio. Some clients may prefer to pay certain vendors (like a printer) directly; however, if they do, you should still receive a services mark-up for overseeing the vendor's work. Some designers prefer to list this mark-up on vendor's services separately as a handling charge, while others simply add the percentage onto the total for each vendor's services.

PRICING COMPUTER-GENERATED WORK

This relatively new area of design is still very hard to price accurately, because technology changes very quickly, and designers are using a whole new set of tools and skills for which they do not have a long history of price comparisons.

Designers are by no means in agreement about how to bill for expenses on computer design jobs. A recent poll of several designers found them charging clients from 50 cents to $7 for a laser printout! As with any design job, it is best to price computer-generated work with an eye to the current price.

To price computer-generated work precisely, you must first consider the final application of the design. Will it be broadcast or printed? How wide an audience will see it? What additional skills are required to produce the work besides your design talents? Your knowledge of computers and design software is essential and valuable to the client, and should be priced accordingly.

Although designing on a computer may save time (revisions can be made almost instantaneously and a rough copy printed out immediately), expenses may be higher in transferring the design to different mediums (e.g., printing slides or film from computer disk or preparing artwork for computer scan). Other additional costs may include rental of support equipment or purchase of additional software for complex design jobs, and consulting fees for technical assistants. You may be able to reduce some costs if production houses can use your design work on diskette instead of them having to enter work into their own system. This results in a lower out-of-pocket expense to you, advantages for you and your client, and higher profits.

UNDERSTANDING YOUR RIGHTS

You should never do any kind of work without a written contract (or signed purchase order). Period. Besides the obvious legal protection that a contract provides you, coming to a detailed, written agreement forces both parties to be perfectly clear and specific about what they want and expect from the deal. When what a buyer and seller are talking about is for the most part intangible at the time of purchase (e.g., a design idea), a written contract ensures that both sides understand as much as they can before agreeing upon the deal. Clarity in the early stages of a design job can save you the emotional and profit-draining trauma of having to make major changes once the design project is underway. If you begin work just having received a signed purchase order, it is important for your protection and the client's that you still sign your contracts as soon as possible once an agreement has been reached. *Don't* accept the excuse from a client that working with a purchase order is okay and is done all the time. You need to spell everything the client expects out for your own protection.

The other reason that even the smallest job should always be backed by a written agreement is that the final value of a design is not always apparent when it's first use is sold. For instance, say you hand-letter a book jacket and are paid $500 for the job. Then, ten years later, the book is made into a movie, and the producers want to use the book lettering on the movie poster and print ads. If it is not clear who owns the rights to the lettering, you may be out a lot more than the original $500 if you cannot prove all rights belong to you.

A contract needn't be full of legal mumbo-jumbo to stand up in court. Technically, it needn't even be in writing, although, of course, verbal agreements are much harder to verify than a written contract. It's just good business practice to have all contracts in writing.

Unless a job is very complicated or involves special circumstances or usage rights, you can usually use a form contract (see samples in this chapter) that you develop yourself or have a lawyer draft for you. Some designers just use a simple bill of sale (see sample on pages 34-35) accompanied by a letter that reiterates the points agreed upon verbally. For example:

"It was a pleasure meeting with you about (project description) on (date). It is my understanding that I will supply you with (design description) on (date), and that you will be buying (describe usage rights) only to this design. I will receive (dollar amount) at the beginning of the job, (dollar amount) when preliminary sketches are approved, and (dollar amount) on the day the design job is completed. If the design project is cancelled through no fault of my own, I will receive the total fee agreed upon for the job. In case of rejection of my design, I will receive 50 percent of the original fee. Please sign the enclosed copy of this letter and return it to me, keeping one copy for your records. I look forward to working with you."

If you often do design jobs of a particular type or types, you might want to draft a contract specifically for those jobs (e.g., a "signage" contract, a "book jacket" contract, etc.)

Often, there are changes that take place during the course of a design job that might merit modifications to the contract. When this is the case, simply draft a letter outlining the new contract information and send it to the client for a signature. For example:

"In addition to the letterhead I am designing for ABC Corporation, we agreed on (date) that I would also create a design using the company logo to be printed onto pens and pencils. I will be paid (dollar amount) for this additional design, payable upon receipt of the final version."

The length and complexity of a formal contract depends upon several factors. In general, it is better to err on the side of including too many clauses than to risk leaving out a crucial one. In drafting a contract for your services, you and your lawyer should consider the following elements:

■ *Payment.* Specify when you will receive payment, advances or royalties, and state the monthly interest that will be charged on any late payments.

■ *Expenses.* Depending on the type and complexity of the design, you may want to stipulate that the client will pay for all expenses incurred in creating the design. If you expect expenses to be large, request an advance

Purchase Order

TO _____ DATE _____

_____

DESCRIPTION OF ASSIGNMENT _____

_____

_____

_____

DELIVERY DATE _____ FEE _____

BUYER SHALL REIMBURSE ARTIST FOR THE FOLLOWING EXPENSES:

_____

_____

_____

_____

_____

THE BUYER PURCHASES THE FOLLOWING EXCLUSIVE RIGHTS OF USAGE:

Title or Product _____

Category of Use_____

Medium of Use_____

Edition (of book)_____

Geographic Area_____

Time Period_____

Artist reserves any usage rights not expressly transferred. Any usage beyond that granted to buyer herein shall require the payment of a mutually agreed upon additional fee, subject to all terms below.

TERMS:

1. TIME FOR PAYMENT. All invoices shall be paid within thirty (30) days of receipt.

2. CHANGES. Buyer shall make additional payments for changes requested in original assignment. However, no additional payment shall be made for changes required to conform to the original assignment description. The Buyer shall offer the Artist first opportunity to make any changes.

3. EXPENSES. Buyer shall reimburse Artist for all expenses arising from this assignment, including but not limited to all those listed above, and the payment of any sales taxes due on this assignment. Buyer's approval shall be obtained for any increases in fees or expenses that exceed the original estimate by 10% or more.

4. CANCELLATION. In the event of cancellation of this assignment, ownership of all copyrights and the original artwork shall be retained by the Artist, and a cancellation fee for work completed, based on the contract price and expenses already incurred, shall be paid by the Buyer.

5. OWNERSHIP OF ARTWORK. The Artist retains ownership of all original artwork, whether preliminary or final, and the Buyer shall return such artwork within thirty (30) days of use.

6. CREDIT LINES. Credit line shall be in the form:

© _____ 19 _____

The Buyer shall give Artist and any other creators a credit line with any editorial usage.

7. RELEASES. Buyer shall indemnify Artist against all claims and expenses, including reasonable attorney's fees, due to uses for which no release was requested in writing or for uses which exceed authority granted by a release.

8. MODIFICATIONS. Modification of the Agreement must be written, except that the invoice may include, and Buyer shall pay, fees or expenses that were orally authorized in order to progress promptly with the work.

_____
ARTIST'S SIGNATURE

_____
COMPANY NAME

_____
AUTHORIZED SIGNATURE

_____
NAME AND TITLE

A purchase order should spell out exactly what the job requires, as well as what reproduction rights are being purchased and which are reserved by the designer. This purchase order is specific about the time for payment and expenses.

© Jean Perwin. The Artist's Friendly Legal Guide (North Light Books, 1988).

against expenses from the client. If you do bill the client for expenses, then an itemized estimate of total expenses should be included in the original agreement. As the project progresses, any expenditure that will exceed your estimate should be approved in advance by the client.

■ *Assumptions.* It is important in any contract to list all assumptions that must hold true in order for all other clauses to be fulfilled, such as maximum number of days allowed for the client to review and approve work, maximum number of changes that can be requested within the agreed upon budget, etc. These are especially important if you are working on a fixed price job rather than billing for time and expenses as they are incurred.

■ *Usage rights.* You should copyright any designs you create. Legally, you have copyright as soon as you create a design, but you should place notice on the work (© plus your name and the year) to make your ownership of it explicit. Since copyright law is different for different types of design, it is in your best interest to look into the ways it applies to your designs. You can obtain more information on copyright from an attorney or from the Copyright Office, Library of Congress, Washington, DC 20559.

Depending on the kind of design you do, a client may be buying exclusive rights to the design, the right to use it only for certain types of products, or just one-time usage. In any case, the client's rights to usage of the design should be clearly stated in the contract; any usage rights not explicitly purchased by the client remain with the designer.

■ *Credits.* If you don't want a design reproduced without a credit line naming you as designer, you must stipulate this in the contract. Depending on the type of design and how it is used, you may want to run a copyright notice as your credit line (© Daphne Designer 1991). If the design would look odd with a credit line, then you may choose to stipulate where else on the page or product your credit must run when the design is reproduced.

■ *Original art and reproductions.* State in your contract that the original design must be returned to you, and that you are entitled to receive at least two copies of the finished piece in which your design was reproduced.

■ *Cancellation.* Cancellation occurs when the job is cancelled through no fault of yours. You should stipulate that if this happens in the middle of a design project, your fee will be paid in proportion to the degree of completion of the design at the time of cancellation, but you must get at least 50 percent of the original fee. If the design is completed but then "cancelled," the client should receive the originally stipulated rights in return for paying you the original fee—even if he no longer wants to use the design.

■ *Rejection.* Rejection occurs when a design is deemed unacceptable. Again, a percentage of the fee that reflects the degree of completion should be paid to you. You should receive between half and one-third of the original amount. In cases of rejection, all rights to the design revert back to the designer, and expenses must be reimbursed in full by the client. If there was a royalty agreement, then the client and designer must negotiate a reasonable fee.

■ *Artistic control.* This is a sticky area that may be hard to cover in a contract, but should be mentioned. Basically, you should ensure that if your design is changed in any way, you must be given a chance to make the changes yourself (and compensated for the extra work) or at least have final approval if someone else works on the design. You might also want to reserve the right to remove your design credit from a project if you feel the final design is too far from the one you created to be called yours.

■ *Arbitration.* Disputes settled by an arbitration panel are enforceable by law, just like regular court decisions. However, unlike judges or a jury, an arbitration panel for any design dispute must have expertise and experience in the design field. Since many designers feel a knowledge of the design industry is necessary in order to render a fair decision in a contract or payment dispute over their work, they would prefer arbitration over a regular court trial. Given that arbitration must be agreed to by both parties, you might want to include a clause in your standard contract that stipulates any dispute must be settled by arbitration. As your client signs the contract, you will automatically gain the other party's consent.

For further advice on how to draft a form contract, consult *The Artist's Friendly Legal Guide* by Floyd Conner et al. (North Light Books, 1988). The American Institute of Graphic Arts (AIGA) has drafted the first form contract specifically for graphic artists. Even if you can't use it as is, you may still want to examine a copy for ideas about what to include in your contracts. (See the Resources section at the end of this book for AIGA's address.)

HOW AND WHEN TO BILL

Selling designs is a little different from selling other products, such as cars or blenders. For the most part, the value of the design lies exclusively in its worth to the company or person for whom you designed it—in other words, you typically cannot recoup a loss by "repossessing" a design for nonpayment. Of course, you *can* make usage rights contingent upon payment in full, which is, in effect, a way of "repossessing" the design, but it is better for your business if you don't have to resort to such drastic measures. One way to help protect your studio from taking such losses is to institute an effective billing system.

An accurate and workable recordkeeping system is important not only at tax time but also for billing purposes. Many designers find that keeping a separate job file for each project, which includes all correspondence, receipts, invoices, etc., helps them keep track of who owes them what and when. A good procedure is to send one copy of the invoice to the client, file a second copy in the job file, and put a third copy in a folder marked Accounts Receivable. When the invoice is paid, the copy from the Accounts Receivable folder is marked paid and the amount noted in the general ledger (see

Chapter Four). The two office copies are then stapled together and left in the job file in case they are ever needed to document revenues for tax purposes.

It is also important for the financial management of your studio that you note when payment is received for outstanding invoices. This information can be useful in calculating the average collection period and drawing up a cash flow statement for your studio. (See Chapter Four.)

How you bill a job should depend on the size and nature of the job and on the size and reputation of the client. However, even if you're doing a small job for the most trusted firm in your town, be sure to collect at least a portion of your fee up front. If you don't, then for all practical purposes you are working "on spec," with payment contingent on the acceptance of the design, and that is no way for a professional to run a business.

A good rule of thumb for billing is to require one-third of the total fee on the day the contract is signed, one-third after approval of preliminary sketches, and the final third *on the day* you turn over the final design to the client. That last third is particularly important, since if you have any doubts about a client's willingness or ability to pay you can keep the final design until the check is in your hand. This may sound harsh, but after the first time you've been stiffed for all or part of your fee, it will seem more like common sense.

Every payment you receive should be in response to an invoice. (See an invoice worksheet and a final invoice on pages 38 and 39.) Even if you have agreed upon a payment schedule and you know, for instance, that the client will have a check for you when you meet to go over preliminary sketches, type up an invoice and bring it with you to the meeting. The invoice will assure that both the client's records and your own are correct.

A reasonable time period in which to expect payment in full (if you haven't stipulated otherwise in your contract) is thirty days after you have turned over a design to a client. In fact, many designers stipulate at the bottom of their

I   N   V   O   I   C   E

attn: _____   CMN job number: _____

to: _____   job name: _____

_____

_____   invoice date: _____ *n/a* *

_____   client's po number: _____

description: _____   fee: _____

_____ $ _____

_____   _____

_____   _____

_____   _____

_____   _____

_____   _____

_____   _____

_____   _____

_____   _____

author's alterations : design   _____

            : typesetting   _____

please list itemized add'l charges below, if applicable / **note: these charges should reflect mark-up.**

_____ $ _____

_____   _____

_____   _____

_____   _____

_____   _____

_____   _____

_____   _____

_____   _____

_____   subtotal $ _____ *n/a* *

        ○ yes   ○ no   sales tax $ _____ *n/a* *

                       total due $ _____ *n/a* *

                          discount $ _____ *n/a* *

* please disregard all blanks labeled n/a.

Corey
McPherson
Nash

9 GALEN STREET
WATERTOWN
MASSACHUSETTS
02172
617 924 6050
FAX: 923 0857

Corey & Company: Designers, Inc.

Corey Edmonds Millen — New York

Corey McPherson Nash — Boston

I N V O I C E

Attn:

To:

Invoice Number:

Job Name:

Invoice Date:

Description   Fee

The form on page 38 is used by Corey & Co. Designers as an invoice worksheet to record expenses as they are incurred. The final figure is transferred to the invoice on this page, which is then sent to the client.

Total Due:

Discount:

Please make check payable to Corey & Company: Designers
9 Galen Street, Watertown, Massachusetts 02172
Terms: Net 30 days. 1½% per month on unpaid balances after 30 days.
Discount: 2% for payment by _____

invoice form that any unpaid balance after thirty days will be charged 1.5 percent interest per month, for an annualized rate of 18 percent (about equal to that of a typical credit card). This is not a bad idea, considering the costs to you of sending repeated invoices, keeping track of overdue accounts, and the interest you could have been earning on the money.

You should check with your accountant or attorney about the maximum interest charge you can assess for late payments. Interest charges vary from state to state. You should also include a clause in your contract stating that you intend to assess a late fee proportionate to any overdue amount. (The billing checklist on page 41 should provide help in remembering *all* costs to bill for.)

WHAT TO DO WHEN CLIENTS DON'T PAY

For many people, pursuing a slow-to-pay client is a terribly difficult experience. They feel embarrassed, indignant, used and annoyed, all at once. If and when you do have to handle the unpleasant task of collecting an overdue account, it may help to keep in mind that unpaid fees are a direct bite taken out of your studio's profits. Not just a loss of revenue, but a direct reduction in your total profit because the expenditures associated with the design have already been made. The money comes right out of your pocket.

It is important to remember that any time you are producing a design for a client and you have not yet been paid in full, you are in effect a "creditor" to that client. Think about it: If you met someone for the first time in a business meeting and at the end of the meeting he asked you to loan him $7,000, you probably wouldn't do it. But you may meet with a client once, agree on a $10,000 design job, and then complete most of it with only a $3,000 payment up front. In effect, you "loan" the client $7,000.

In collecting payment from resistant clients, an ounce of prevention really can be worth a pound of cure. Use common sense: If you were to loan someone money, wouldn't you make sure to find out his home address and phone

number, bank, nearest relative, and even ask for references? The same information should be collected when you take on a new client, unless, of course, the client is a large company that cannot "vanish" easily. Business stationery stores sell generic "credit application" forms that you can ask a new client to complete. If you are concerned that a credit application might put people off because it seems formal, then just make sure to get the following information from a new client in a more informal way:

- Business name and address.
- Home and business telephone numbers.
- Former address.
- Former employers.
- Business's monthly income.
- Bank branch, and savings and checking account numbers.
- Spouse's name and where employed.
- Names of any other officers or principals in the company.
- The names and telephone numbers of three other creditors (e.g., suppliers, bank loan officers).

This information can be vital in helping to weed out potential deadbeats and in finding them if they leave part of your fee unpaid.

Collecting Overdue Payments

You should develop a collection procedure for your studio that includes regularly scheduled mailings of invoices and collection letters, plus telephone calls when needed. Assuming your contracts do *not* stipulate that payment in full is due on the day the design is delivered, use

Since Corey & Co. Designers of Boston doesn't use a purchase order system, the firm uses a billing checklist to keep track of expenses. Expenses that are figured into an initial quote for a job are listed under "exp.", while additional expenses are listed under "aa's". Using the checklist insures that all invoices are filed and also keeps tabs on how much time and money being spent is on a job.

B I L L I N G   C H E C K L I S T

job title:	pd:	quoted?
number:		○ partial billing
attention:		○ final billing
client:		
address:		

Corey McPherson Nash

9 GALEN STREET
WATERTOWN
MASSACHUSETTS
02172
617 924 6050
FAX: 923 0857

	exp.	aa's	vendor	amount
art supplies	○	○		
color seps	○	○		
copywriting	○	○		
delivery	○	○		
entertainment	○	○		
illustration	○	○		
photography	○	○		
printing	○	○		
stats	○	○		
travel / taxi	○	○		
typesetting	○	○		
xeroxes	○	○		
mac	○	○		
other	○	○		
other	○	○		
last day working				

bill: [check and fill in amount]

○ quote	○ aa's	○ add'l.
○ actual		
sales tax? ○ no ○ yes		
description:		

the following procedure to pursue slow-to-pay clients:

Step 1. Two weeks after you submit the design (with your invoice), send another invoice reminding the client of the 30-day deadline, after which a finance charge will be levied.

Step 2. Ten days after the 30-day deadline has passed, consider the bill overdue, and make the first phone call. State politely but firmly that the deadline for payment has passed, and that you'd like to know when you can expect payment.

Step 3. Based on the client's reaction, your judgment as to the likelihood of imminent payment, and your willingness to jeopardize future relationships with the same client, you should call and send increasingly firm letters with regularity. Be clear about your expectations: "I'm sure you want to clear this matter up, so we will need to receive your check by Wednesday the 23rd at 5 P.M. to avoid turning your account over to a collection agency." But don't make these statements if you are not prepared to carry them out, or you won't be taken seriously.

Step 4. At seventy-five days overdue, it is time to make a decision about whether to pursue the matter further. If the amount is large enough to make it worth your while, you may want to hire a collection agency. Keep in mind, however, that an agency's fee is usually 40 percent to 50 percent of the amount collected. You can also sue the client in small claims or regular court. But consider the costs of doing so: emotional wear and tear, time spent away from your design business, and legal costs. Sometimes you may be better off just swallowing the loss, and strengthening your resolve to ask for more of your fee up front and to do a more thorough credit check of an "iffy" client's credit history next time.

There's one factor that can help you greatly in collecting an overdue payment—knowing *why* a client hasn't paid. If at all possible, talk with the person who is responsible for making the payment. Find out if the client is strapped for cash, unhappy with the design, or just plain forgetful. If you listen, you may be able to reason with the client, resolve any complaints, and even offer an alternative payment schedule or amount.

If the debt is grave enough to warrant hiring a collection agency, choose a reputable outfit. The Fair Debt Collection Practices Act protects debtors from undue harassment in debt collection, and if you hire an agency that uses dubious tactics, you may be held responsible for their actions under the law. For a list of approved agencies in your area, contact the American Collectors Association, 4040 W. 70th St., Minneapolis, MN 55435, 612-926-6547.

CHAPTER THREE
TROUBLESHOOTERS

Q. *A client for whom I just did a design job, and from whom I hope to get more work, is questioning the way I bill expenses. He points out that since I bill for my labor separately, I shouldn't also add on a 17 percent mark-up for expenses from outside vendors. I know this is standard, but how can I justify the charge?*

A. You most certainly should be billing the client a 15 percent to 20 percent mark-up on vendor services. Explain to your client that this percentage covers your time in finding the best quality and prices for various outside services and supervising the vendors that provide them. The labor hours you bill for cover research and design time only, not time spent dealing with vendors. If a client had to find and check the work of illustrators, photographers, printers, and other vendors himself, it would cost him a lot more than the 17 percent mark-up you're charging for that service.

Q. *A client for whom I was designing a new letterhead declared bankruptcy the day before I was to meet her with preliminary sketches. I got one-third of my fee up front, but the cancellation clause in my contract says I should be paid at least 50 percent of the total fee if the design job is cancelled (and I assume bankruptcy = cancellation in this case). What should I do?*

A. Like all of her creditors, you will be paid all or some of what the client owes you depending on the bankruptcy plan that the court devises. Just make sure that the trustees handling the business know you are owed at least half of your fee, minus the third you were wise enough to get up front.

Q. *I recently underpriced a job because I underestimated typography costs by quite a bit. I let the client know about the added expense, and he was very disgruntled, but agreed to pay it. I'm now afraid that I've lost any chance of getting more business from him. Any suggestions?*

A. This is one of the reasons that the "assumptions" section of your contract is important. In it, you might include a phrase about who shares the burden if standard rates rise after you've done the pricing estimate. Although it's not a good idea to make it a practice, in this case you might want to reduce your vendor mark-up on the expense that you underestimated. Coming down from, say, 15 percent to 10 percent, and pointing this out to the client, will show that you are sharing in some of the cost of your mistake.

CHAPTER THREE
CHECKLISTS

To set an hourly rate:
- ☐ Divide total annual overhead by 1,000 hours for principals.
- ☐ Divide an employee's total annual salary by 1,500 for an hourly employee rate.

For setting standard job rates:
- ☐ Set different rates for different job types.
- ☐ Consult your old job files.
- ☐ Check with colleagues.
- ☐ Price print work as a percentage of the advertising page rate for the publication.

Job pricing methods include:
- ☐ The overhead/hourly rate method.
- ☐ The market rate method.
- ☐ The itemized pricing method.

Points to consider when pricing a job:
- ☐ Usage rights.
- ☐ Licensing and royalties.
- ☐ Complexity of design.
- ☐ Steady or larger projects.
- ☐ Short deadlines.
- ☐ Circulation.
- ☐ Consultations.
- ☐ Taxes.
- ☐ Vendor's services mark-up.

When pricing computer-generated work:
- ☐ Consider the design's application and circulation.
- ☐ Add expenses for technical assistance and transferring designs between mediums.
- ☐ Charge for the added skill of software and computer knowledge.

When you have agreed to accept a job, remember that:
- ☐ All design jobs should be backed with a written agreement.
- ☐ Small jobs may be able to be covered with a more informal contract/letter.
- ☐ Develop standard contract types for different kinds of design jobs.
- ☐ All contracts should be signed by both parties, even letter contracts.
- ☐ Simple jobs (or minor changes to jobs) should be verified in a contract letter.

Your contract should cover:
- ☐ Payment.
- ☐ Expenses.
- ☐ Assumptions.
- ☐ Usage rights.
- ☐ Credits.
- ☐ Return of original art and reproductions for your portfolio.
- ☐ Cancellation.
- ☐ Rejection.
- ☐ Artistic control.
- ☐ Arbitration.

How and when to bill:
- ☐ Set up billing on a regular monthly or semi-monthly basis.
- ☐ Bill one-third up front, one-third after preliminary sketches, and one-third when the job is completed or as your contract stipulates.
- ☐ Always make out an invoice for each payment you are due to receive.
- ☐ Charge interest on payments after thirty days:

Collecting overdue payment:
- [ ] Remember that you are a client's creditor.
- [ ] New clients should complete a credit information form that lists:
  - Business name and address.
  - Home and business telephone numbers.
  - Former address.
  - Former employers.
  - Business's monthly income.
  - Bank branch, checking and savings account numbers.
  - Spouse's name and place of employment.
  - Names of officer or principals in the company.
  - Credit references.
- [ ] Develop a collection procedure for your studio.
- [ ] Find out *why* a client hasn't paid.
- [ ] Drop the collection effort if it becomes too costly.
- [ ] Ask the American Collectors Association to recommend a collection agency.

CHAPTER 4

KEEP THE CASH FLOWING

PROFIT POINTS

Capitalize on the strength of every dollar you make by:

- Recognizing your true "financial" colors.
- Keeping track of where your money comes from and where it goes.
- Choosing the right accounting method.
- Knowing when to spend money to make money.

Even though you may prefer to pay an accountant to handle the books, you should always be aware of your studio's financial position. In order to understand how your business is doing, you need a firm grasp of the accounting basics used to chart a business's fiscal progress. If you don't understand the framework, then it really is all just a meaningless bunch of numbers for you.

This chapter is designed to explain that framework to you. It will help you understand where and when cash is coming into and going out of your studio, how to make decisions about expanding your business, how much cash you should keep in the bank, and how to estimate your studio's profitability. Most importantly, it should encourage you to take a more active role in financial planning for your studio, and help you learn the tools that will allow you to make informed decisions and boost profits for your design business.

HOW TO KEEP TRACK OF WHERE YOUR MONEY IS GOING

The general financial management of your studio should include:

- Managing existing assets and resources (cash, equipment, property, staff) so they make the maximum contribution to your studio's profits.
- Deciding if your studio can and should acquire new assets or resources (e.g., purchase equipment, take on staff).
- Getting loans or other funds with which to pay for additional assets or resources.
- Repaying the loans used to take on new assets or resources with the profits generated by those new assets or resources.

These are the kinds of tasks you can and should be doing for your studio. With the use of the simple financial management/accounting tools we'll discuss, you can identify and correct the financial imbalances that may be draining away your studio's hard-earned profits. Even if you have an accountant, bookkeeper or business manager who crunches the numbers for you, you need to know how to analyze those numbers to obtain the information needed to make solid financial decisions.

There are three principal tools used to manage a studio's finances:

- *Accounting records.* Whether you keep the records yourself or have someone else do it, the system should be complete, accurate, standardized, and easy to understand.
- *Financial statements.* The two most important of these are the *balance sheet* and the *profit and loss statement* (also called an *income statement*). These statements are the basis for most of the financial analyses that are important to a design studio. They are also the records that provide the information needed to compute quarterly tax payments. And equally important, they are the financial statements any investor or banker will want to see before giving your studio a business loan or investing in it.
- *Analysis techniques.* These are methods of analysis that help you understand whether your studio is running profitably. For instance, one analysis technique divides total current assets by total current liabilities. Using this so-called "current ratio," you can see whether or not you are likely to have enough cash on hand to pay the bills coming due within the next twelve months. (More on this ratio later.)

All three of these tools are useful, and will be described in detail later on in this chapter. But before we get into the nuts and bolts of good financial management, there are a few general rules of accounting and bookkeeping that you should know:

PERSONAL PROFILE

CHERYL HARRISON
Harrison Design Group
San Francisco, California

"I never thought of myself as a person with a 'business-like' mind," says Cheryl Harrison, president and creative director of Harrison Design Group in San Francisco. "But in the ten years since I started the company, I've slowly gotten into the financial management of it, and I've learned quite a bit about accounting and making financial decisions. Little by little, I've become much more interested and involved, and now I'm helping to design an accounting software system for other designers. The ones on the market now aren't really great for handling the multiple jobs that most designers have going at once."

In its ten-year history, Harrison Design Group has evolved from a firm mostly handling image development to one heavily involved in advertising work, and more recently in the relatively new field of environmental design. Its clients are mostly located on the West Coast, and its industry focus is real estate firms, although its client list includes companies nationwide in a variety of industries. Bank of America Corporate Real Estate, Cushman-Wakefield, Howard Hughes Properties, and The Shorenstein Company are among the studio's larger clients. One recent design job for The Shorenstein Company included designing a master signage system for the San Francisco high-rise apartment buildings that the company owns.

Harrison Design Group is a small but busy studio. In addition to creative director Cheryl Harrison, the firm employs one designer/production artist, a director of marketing, an administrative information manager, a production manager, and an administrative assistant, plus an intern, usually from one of the Bay Area colleges.

Although Harrison's first and foremost interest will always be design, the business end of running Harrison Design Group has become increasingly intriguing to her. She has an orderly and fairly efficient accounting system set up for her studio using MultiLedger software, made by CheckMark. When an invoice is received, it is first matched to the purchase order (to make sure the item isn't overcharged or double-billed). Then, the invoice is coded with a number that identifies the job to which the expense relates and the type of item purchased (e.g., "#T48907" indicates typography for job #48907, and all brochure design jobs are given numbers beginning with 48, so expenses can be totaled by either job type or expense type by just looking at their numbers). With this system, Harrison can tell at a glance how much she spends a year on each kind of item, and what the expense total on each job included.

She notes, "This kind of information is vital. For instance, if I notice that certain jobs involve a large number of stats, and we're sending out for all of the stats, then I may decide to buy a stat camera based on the volume of stats we seem to need, especially if we plan on doing more of those types of jobs. Because if we produce the stats in-house, then any profits made off of them go to us instead of the outside stat producer. And we can pass some of those savings on to our clients as well."

The other advantage of an invoice tracking system like Harrison Design Group's is that you can calculate per-job profits and then see quite easily which types of projects are pulling in the most profits for your studio. Since expenses are coded according to the jobs for which they are incurred, you can tell which types of jobs have the highest profit

■ Never take money out of daily cash receipts for your personal use. Pay yourself a salary instead. Your salary should be a fixed amount (like rent or any other fixed business cost); this is easier to keep track of than sporadic withdrawals of cash.

■ Keep a business bank account for all of your studio's funds, and deposit all checks into it on the day you receive them. Large amounts of cash that won't be needed for several months or longer should be shifted to a higher yielding money market account or CD.

margins, and then plan your studio's expansion into new areas accordingly.

While to many designers such a recordkeeping system may sound ideal, Harrison has her sights set even higher. She is working with a computer programmer and her accountant to design an even more sophisticated system for tracking expenses. She says, "The system we're developing is an Excel database that would bill expenses directly to the project for which they are incurred. In this system, when a job's cost is estimated and the job set up, the cost estimate would be broken down into different categories like staff time, color separation, typography, etc. Then as each expense is incurred and billed, the amount would be automatically subtracted from the total in the estimate. By checking the current job status, you could also check whether costs are running over budget, and if so, in which area. Then you could readjust the estimate and let the client know, and also keep an eye on that category so that it wouldn't have to be adjusted upward again."

This isn't all a bunch of useless number crunching. Harrison uses the financial reports this thorough recordkeeping produces to make all kinds of key business decisions. "I always look at income statements and balance sheets before making any kind of decision to add staff or equipment. It helps to know that the numbers are solid, and that we can truly afford to take on a new expense. But I must admit, I'm still not comfortable going into debt to expand the studio. Even though I know you can end up *increasing* profits by investing borrowed money in staff and assets, I don't make any expenditures unless I have the cash on hand. So, despite all of my high-tech accounting methods, my approach to financial management might still be considered old-fashioned."

■ Record all incoming checks—how much, from whom they were received, and the date—on the day you receive them.

■ Pay all suppliers and salaries by check through your business account or from a petty cash fund, never out of daily cash receipts. Set up a petty cash fund for small daily expenses

(taxi fare, small supplies) by writing a check (for $50 to $100) from your business account to "Petty Cash" and putting the cash in a cash box. Note how much you spend, the date, and what it went for on each receipt returned as justification for the petty cash. When petty cash gets low, write a check to the fund for exactly the amount you have used up (total the amounts noted in your petty cash logbook) to bring the total back to the original sum.

■ Have a certified public accountant (CPA) check your financial records every quarter, or at least once a year.

THE FIVE BASIC ACCOUNTING RECORDS

There are five basic elements of your business for which you should keep records. They are as follows:

■ *Sales records.* Monthly statements and itemized invoices are crucial in making projections of future income for your studio, and for designing marketing or promotional plans. It's best to subdivide these sales records into categories that provide useful information about the sales. For instance, if you're interested in the percentage of your total revenues that come from different types of design jobs, divide invoices into categories by job type (e.g., print ad design, logo and corporate identity work, book jacket design, etc.). Then you can go back and see which types of design jobs constitute the largest share of your business. You may also want to categorize by geographic area (if you're trying to expand your market in certain areas), or by the client's business (if you're aiming to get more clients from the same field).

■ *Accounts receivable.* These are client invoices for which you have not yet been paid. It is important to keep track of accounts receivable for two reasons: to be able to take prompt action when invoices become seriously overdue, and to know when to expect more cash coming in so you can pay your own suppliers. If you're not paying attention to accounts receivable, you won't have a good idea of when to expect payment, and without this information, you can't analyze your studio's financial position accurately. If, for instance, you're not aware that large payments are due in a few days, you may become needlessly concerned about upcoming bills.

■ *Cash receipts.* Simply put, cash receipts are records of what money has come in, and from where. Detailed deposit slips for your business checking account can be used to keep an eye on cash flow.

■ *Accounts payable.* These are the bills you receive from suppliers that you have not yet paid. Simply put, it is not a good business practice to pay off bills from suppliers as soon as they arrive. As long as you hold on to that cash, you are effectively getting an interest-free loan from your suppliers, and the more cash you have on hand, the more liquid your business is. Greater liquidity means that you can meet financial emergencies more easily, and have to take on less "investment" debt (like bank loans) in the long run.

This is not to say that you should alienate suppliers by making them wait a long time for payment. What you should do is file bills into weekly "for payment" files. For instance, if a bill arrives on the 10th of the month, put it into a file of bills to be paid during the first week of the next month. That way, you know the bill will be paid within thirty days, which is the normal waiting period for most invoices. Each Friday, take out the appropriate "for payment" file for that week and pay all of the bills in it.

■ *Cash disbursements.* These are any monies paid out by your business. Be sure to write a check out of your business account, and in a ledger list the date, check number, amount, and what the money was for. There are several business checkwriting systems in which the check stub is integrated into a ledger so that you need only write the information once.

KEEPING TRACK OF EVERYDAY EXPENSES

This is the most comprehensive accounting record a studio has. The main purpose of a general ledger is to record *every* monetary transaction that takes place in your business. It contains information about assets, liabilities,

capital, sales and expenses for the entire fiscal year. When you sit down with a pile of receipts and invoices at the end of the day or week, the general ledger is where you record each one. The financial information your studio's general ledger contains provides the building blocks from which all of your other financial management tools (income statements, balance sheets, cash flow statements, etc.) are developed.

An accountant should help you to set up the categories for your general ledger and explain which items belong where. Typical categories that appear in a design studio's general ledger include:

■ *Assets:* Cash in banks, petty cash fund, accounts receivable, inventory of materials and supplies, prepaid expenses, tools and equipment.

■ *Liabilities and owner's equity:* Accounts payable, sales tax payable, FICA (Social Security) tax payable, federal and state withholding and unemployment taxes payable, long-term debt and mortgages, owner's equity.

■ *Revenues and expenses:* Sales, miscellaneous income, salaries and wages, contract labor, payroll taxes, supplies, utilities, rent, postage, insurance, interest, depreciation, and advertising.

Note that a general ledger records assets, liabilities, owner's equity, revenues and expenses. Numbers are not subtracted from each other in a general ledger; they are simply tallied by category for use in other financial management statements.

FINANCIAL STATEMENTS

Measuring What You've Really Earned

Financial statements are the second type of financial management tool you'll use in your studio. As we noted earlier, the two most important of these for a small studio are the *income (profit and loss) statement* and the *balance sheet.*

An income statement (see page 52) measures expenses against revenues over a definite period of time (usually a month, a quarter or a year) to show the net profit (or loss) for the business during the time the statement covers. By examining this statement, you should get a solid idea of·whether or not you are operating as profitably as you'd like to be, and which expenses may be draining hard-earned profits.

The first entry on the income statement is *gross sales* or *revenue* (total income for designs sold). This number includes cash sales as well as amounts due from clients in accounts receivable. The next line is used for allowances for "bad debt," (the percentage of revenues in accounts receivable that you expect won't be paid for) and is subtracted from gross sales to get net sales.

The next entry, *cost of sales*, is rarely used for design businesses because they do not keep an inventory of ready-to-sell products (like a manufacturing business would). Since this amount will be 0, subtract 0 from net sales to get the gross profit (the next line on the income statement). Gross profit is your studio's profit before subtracting operating expenses, interest and taxes.

Operating expenses are the next items on the income statement. Divide them into three categories: 1. Salaries and benefits (for yourself and your employees), 2. General and administrative expenses (supplies, insurance, rent, etc.), and 3. Depreciation (a portion of the cost of equipment purchased either in the period or in the past, that has been allocated to the period). Total the three categories and subtract them from gross profit.

The next line, *other income and expenses,* should be used to tally income or expenses that are not generated directly by the usual running of your studio—for instance, interest earned on cash invested in CDs, and interest paid on loans. Once you've added (or subtracted) net other income (or losses) you get your studio's pretax income.

On the next line, subtract *income taxes*. The resulting amount is your studio's after-tax income. There is one final entry on the income

statement for *extraordinary gains* or *losses.* Use this line to factor in the income or costs derived from a truly unusual occurrence, such as gain on the sale of a valuable piece of real estate when your studio changes location, or loss due to theft. The final line of the income statement shows your *net income* or *loss* for the period it covers.

Charting Your Financial Health
Using your studio's balance sheet (see page 53), you can gauge the financial health of your business at a single point in time. The balance sheet measures the "book value" of your studio on the day on which the balance is tallied and *only* on that day (usually the last day of the month). The market value of your business is probably quite a bit greater than its book value because intangible assets such as your reputation aren't counted on the balance sheet.

The balance sheet is divided into two main sections: 1. Assets, and 2. Liabilities plus owner's equity. The total assets always equal the combined total of the liabilities and the owner's equity (an amount that fluctuates according to the current worth of the business). Because the two numbers balance out, this financial report is called a balance sheet.

Assets on the balance sheet are divided into two main categories:

■ *Current.* Current assets are those that are fairly liquid. Some examples are: cash, accounts receivable, bank deposits, temporary investments (to be cashed in within twelve months), and prepaid expenses.

■ *Long-term (or fixed).* These are assets that cannot readily be transformed into cash. Some examples are: property and equipment that are owned by the business, plus stocks, bonds and bank certificates of deposits of over one-year maturity.

Liabilities are divided into two main categories:

INCOME STATEMENT

Gross Sales (Revenue)		200,000
Allowance for Bad Debt		- 6,000
Net Sales (Revenues)		194,000
Cost of Sales		- 0
Gross Profit		194,000
Operating Expenses:		
Salaries and Benefits	114,000	
General and Administrative	+ 55,000	
Depreciation	+ 5,000	
Other	+ 5,000	
Total Operating Expenses	179,000	-179,000
Operating Profit		15,000
Other Income and Expenses		
Interest Income	+ 4,000	
Interest Expense	- 2,000	
Other Expense	- 3,000	
Other Expense, Net	- 1,000	- 1,000
Pretax Profit		14,000
Income Tax		- 4,900
Net Profit		+ 9,100

An income statement measures expenses against revenues over a definite period of time, usually a month, a quarter, or a year. It shows the net profit (or loss) for the business during the period covered. The income statement gives you a good idea whether you're operating as profitably as you'd like and what expenses might be draining your profits. Note that the cost of sales line, which is zero in this example, measures depletion of inventory. Most design businesses do not have an "inventory" of designs; thus, the cost of sales in this example is 0.

BALANCE SHEET

Assets
Current Assets

Cash	9,000	
Accounts Receivable	+133,000	
Bank Deposits	+ 22,000	
Temporary Investments	+ 20,000	
Prepaid Expenses	+ 5,000	
Total Current Assets	189,000	189,000

Long-term Assets

Gross Property, Plant and Equipment	36,000		
Accumulated Depreciation	- 19,000		
Net Property, Plant and Equipment	17,000	17,000	
Other Investments		+ 42,000	
Total Long-term Assets		59,000	+ 59,000
Total Assets			248,000

Liabilities and Owner's Equity
Current Liabilities

Accounts Payable	116,000	
Notes Payable	+ 11,000	
Salaries Payable	+ 43,000	
Interest Payable	+ 1,000	
Taxes Payable	+ 6,000	
Total Current Liabilities	177,000	177,000

Long-term Liabilities

Long-term Debt	9,000	
Other Long-term Liabilities	+ 15,000	
Total Long-term Liabilities	24,000	+ 24,000

Owner's Equity

Paid-in Capital	4,000	
Retained Earnings	+ 43,000	
Total Owner's Equity	+ 47,000	+ 47,000
Total Liabilities and Owner's Equity		248,000

A balance sheet is an itemized statement listing the total assets and total liabilities of a business. It reports the business's "book value" (or "owner's equity") at a given moment. It does not usually list intangibles, such as the value of your design talent, which should be considered in appraising the total market value of your studio.

■ *Current.* Current liabilities are those that you must pay within one year. Accounts payable, notes payable (the balance of the principal due on short-term loans), payroll, interest payable, and taxes payable.

■ *Long-term.* These are your longer term liabilities, like the remaining principal on all debts due over a period exceeding one year.

The difference between total assets and total liabilities is called the net worth or owner's equity. Basically, this number tells you the studio's net worth on a given day. A studio's net worth or owner's equity will fluctuate as asset and liability totals fluctuate. If you are a sole proprietor, the owner's equity is the current book value (not market value; see distinction on page 51) of your investment. In a partnership or corporation, of course, ownership of the equity is divided up among the partners or shareholders according to their shares in the business. Owner's equity is also reduced by the amount paid out to the owners (via partnership distributions or corporate dividends).

One of the many uses of a balance sheet can be to help you apply for a bank loan for your studio. By examining your studio's balance sheet, (along with its income and cash flow statements), a banker will be able to gauge your ability to pay back the loan. Your owner's equity may serve as collateral for a business loan.

HOW TO SEE WHERE THE CASH FLOWS

A cash flow statement (see page 55) is another type of financial report you must construct for your studio. It can be prepared using information from the general ledger only, just like the balance sheet and income statement. It is designed to show your studio's net increase (or decrease) in cash over a given period of time (usually a quarter or a year). By reading a cash flow statement, you should be able to see the sources and uses of cash in your business. And, if you examine when and why the cash "flows" in and out, you can gauge whether your studio is being run in a financially sound and profitable manner.

The first part of a cash flow statement calculates cash from operating activities, that is, from the profitable selling of your designs. Net income is recorded on the first line, and then is followed by noncash items affecting net income, such as depreciation and deferred income taxes, and by changes in receivables, inventory or payables. Noncash expenses that were subtracted from revenues on the income statement are added back to operating cash flow, from which cash outflows not included in the income statement, such as an increase in receivables, are subtracted.

The second section covers cash flows from investing. Cash spent to purchase real estate or equipment shows up here, as do the cash proceeds from the sale of old property.

The third section shows cash flows from financing—for example, cash that goes out to pay off long-term debt, or comes in from a new bank loan. Distributions paid out to partners (or dividends paid out to stockholders) also appear here.

After each section is totaled separately, the three section totals are combined; the result is your studio's net increase (or decrease) in cash over the period the statement covers. Even if all of these section totals are occasionally negative, it doesn't necessarily mean your business is suffering. During a business's start-up stage, cash flows from operations and investing are likely to be negative. However, beware that you can run a negative cash flow only as long as you have cash in the bank to cover the outlays. Persistent negative cash flows from operations is a sure danger sign.

CASH OR ACCRUAL: WHICH ACCOUNTING METHOD IS BEST FOR YOU?

There are two basic methods for keeping track of your studio's money.

Cash Accounting

This is the simplest method of accounting and one used by many sole proprietorships and small businesses. To use the cash accounting method, you need only keep track of cash revenues and cash expenses. In other words, an

CASH FLOW STATEMENT

Cash Flow from Operating Activities		
Net Profit	9,100	
Depreciation	5,000	
Deferred Taxes	700	
Other	600	
Changes in:		
Decrease (Increase) in Accounts Receivable	(22,000)	
Increase (Decrease) in Accounts Payable	24,000	
Increase (Decrease) in Notes Payable	2,000	
Increase (Decrease) in Income Taxes Payable	(1,000)	
Net Cash provided by Operating Activities	18,400	18,400
Cash Flow from Investing Activities		
Purchase of Property, Plant and Equipment	(6,000)	
Proceeds from Sale of Assets	1,000	
Other	(4,500)	
Net Cash used in Investing Activities	(9,500)	- 9,500
Cash Flow from Financing Activities		
Long-term Borrowing	3,000	
Payments on Long-term Debt	(1,000)	
Other	(7,000)	
Net Cash used in Financing Activities	(5,000)	- 5,000
Net Increase (Decrease) in Cash		3,900
Cash at Beginning of Year		+25,000
Cash at End of Year		28,900

A cash flow statement shows a studio's net increase or decrease in cash in a given time period. It shows if your business is running in a sound manner. Even though this example shows a negative cash flow in Investing Activities, this is not necessarily a bad sign because it shows that money is being invested in the business. Most studios experience a negative cash flow when they open because they must make major equipment purchases.

expense is noted only when the money is paid out (even if that's thirty days after the purchase occurred), and payment is recorded only when you receive it (even if you completed the design two months ago.)

Since in the design business, most of the cash expenses relating to a project occur during the same quarter in which the cash revenues are received (and almost always during the same year), the cash accounting method doesn't typically distort the profitability picture too much. The major exception is the purchase of real estate or equipment that will be used for several years. It would be distortive, for example, for you to think your studio lost money in a year in which you bought a $10,000 stat camera, if the business would have shown a $10,000 profit not counting the stat camera. If the camera is expected to last five years, you should only expense $2,000 ($10,000 divided by 5) in the current year. Thus, your "true" profit would be $8,000 in that year—not $0.

Accrual Basis Accounting

In the accrual method, each revenue item is entered in the general ledger as it is billed and each expense is entered as it's incurred, without regard to when actual payment is received or made. The advantage of accrual accounting over the cash method is that accrual offers a more accurate picture of your studio's profitability and solvency. You don't run the risk of thinking that your studio is doing much better than it actually is just because you haven't paid all the bills, or that it's doing much worse just because a big client may be a little late with its payment.

If your studio uses the accrual method, its cash flow statement will be especially helpful in tracking the business's day-to-day liquidity. Knowing that your studio is running profitably won't be much consolation if bills must be paid now but cash won't be coming in for several weeks. You need to know in advance when you'll need a short-term loan to tide you over.

An accountant can advise you on which accounting method to use, depending on the size of your business and the types of clients who commission your designs.

LIQUIDITY: KNOWING IF THERE'S CASH ON HAND

Liquidity is the ability to make cash available to your studio as needed. Liquidity is enhanced by having a lot of cash in the bank, by holding assets that can easily be sold for cash, by having a strong operating cash flow, and/or by having ample credit lines available from banks. Usually, the higher the liquidity of your studio, the better, although there are points at which this does not hold true. Although liquid-

ity is important, it's also expensive. If you have too much cash lying around uninvested, you are missing out on opportunities to acquire resources and assets (more staff, better equipment) that could be making your studio more money. So, you must strike a balance. You should keep a reserve of cash just large enough to carry you through financial rough spots, but reinvest all the cash you can back into the studio to further boost profits. The best idea if you are 'cash rich' is to consult your accountant who can advise you of the best balance for your studio.

Using the information from the financial statements described previously (income statement, balance sheet, general ledger, and cash flow statement), you should be able to calculate the ratios detailed below and in doing so, get a much better idea of your studio's liquidity. These ratios are a few of the "analysis techniques" described earlier in this chapter as the third kind of financial management tool.

The Current Ratio

This ratio shows whether your current assets (cash, accounts receivable and inventories) can cover your current liabilities (accounts payable, payroll, taxes payable, and rent due) with a safety margin for unforeseen losses such as nonpayment of some accounts receivable. Using the information on your balance sheet, divide current assets by current liabilities. A sound current ratio for a design studio (because a studio rarely has inventories) is typically around 1.5:1 (current assets:current liabilities). If your current ratio is too low, you can raise it by converting noncurrent (illiquid) assets into liquid ones (e.g., selling a piece of equipment and depositing the proceeds from the sale in the studio's bank account), by borrowing more money long-term to pay down some of the short-term liabilities, or by funneling a larger percentage of operating cash flow into current assets (or the repayment of current liabilities), rather than into the purchase of long-term assets (or the repayment of long-term debt).

Here is an example of how to compute your current ratio:

$$\frac{\text{Current Assets}}{\text{Current Liabilities}} = \frac{189,000}{177,000} = 1.06:1$$

The Average Collection Period

This calculation can be very helpful in charting cash flow and liquidity. The average collection period is the number of days between when you bill for a design job and when you collect the money for it. You can use your income statement to calculate it. Take your net sales and divide them by the number of days the statement covers (30, 90, or 365). The result is average sales per day. Then from your balance sheet, take the total accounts receivable and divide it by the average sales per day. The resulting number is the number of days in your average collection period.

This can be expressed as:

$$\frac{\text{Net Sales}}{\text{Number of Days}} = \text{Average Sales}$$

$$\frac{\text{Accounts Receivable}}{\text{Average Sales}} = \text{Average Collection Period}$$

Since the typical collection period for designers is thirty days, an average collection period of more than forty days would indicate a problem you should look into. (See Chapter Three for more on how to get paid on time.)

WHEN YOUR STUDIO SHOULD TAKE ON DEBT

You will probably reach the point when you realize there is enough work to justify expanding your business, and you will have to fund the expansion. After analyzing your studio's financial statement, you may realize that you have sufficient cash on hand (and cash flowing in regularly) to finance your projected expansion (taking on staff, buying equipment) with your studio's own money.

But more likely, you will need to borrow money to purchase new equipment or make some other business expansion. In deciding how much you can afford to borrow for an expansion, you must try to project the extra profits you will learn as a result of the new investments you are making, and then determine whether these extra profits will more than offset the cost of financing the loans you will need to pay for the new asset. Let's go through an example:

You should use the following steps to decide whether a new asset will be a good investment for your studio. (See chart on page 58.) Assume that you are considering buying a personal computer and design software.

1. *Determine the annualized cost of the equipment.* The equipment costs $10,000. You plan to take out a five-year bank loan to pay for it, and to depreciate it over five years. Its estimated resale value after five years will be $1,500. Subtract its resale value ($1,500) from its total cost ($10,000), and divide the result by the five years to get the annualized cost of the equipment ($10,000 - $1,500 = $8,500 divided by 5 = $1,700 per year).

2. *Calculate the tax savings from interest to be paid.* The interest on the five-year loan is 15 percent of the total ($1,500) per year. This interest is deductible from your business income on your tax return, so your tax bill is lowered by $1,500 × your tax bracket, say 30 percent. So you save $450 in taxes ($1,500 × 30 percent tax bracket or .3 = $450).

3. *Calculate the tax savings from additional depreciation.* By depreciating the equipment over five years, you lower pretax business profits by $1,700 each year, and this reduction in profits results in an additional tax savings of $510 ($1,700 × 30 percent tax bracket or .3 = $510).

4. *Tally the real annualized cost of the equipment.* The real cost to your studio per year for this new computer is $1,700 + $1,500 - $450 - $510 = $2,240. In order to be clear, this example assumes that all principal is repaid when the loan matures rather than in parts periodically, which is more typical.

5. *Calculate whether the additional profits*

Cost of equipment	$10,000
Resale value after 5 years	- 1,500
	8,500
$8,500 divided by 5 years	1,700
Financing costs of the loan (per year)	+ 1,500
Total yearly cost of the equipment	3,200
Tax savings from interest	- 450
	2,750
Tax savings from additional depreciation	- 510
Real annualized cost of the equipment	2,240

This example shows how you can determine whether or not a major purchase would be profitable. The designer must decide if it would be wise to buy a computer for $10,000. Her first step is to calculate the real, annualized cost of the equipment, which would be $2,240. To decide whether or not the purchase is wise, she must then estimate the incremental profitability gained by using the computer in her business and see if it will exceed the effective cost.

generated by the new computer system will more than cover its real cost. Estimate how much more yearly revenue the equipment will generate, and then subtract the added annual costs of the labor, supplies, and studio overhead (such as utilities) that the additional work will use. Subtract taxes, and the number you get will give you a rough idea of the new equipment's potential for producing extra profits. To benefit your studio, these profits should exceed or at least cover the cost of the equipment per year.

HOW TO MEASURE YOUR STUDIO'S PROFITABILITY

There are many different analysis techniques for calculating profitability. For a design business, the most useful gauges are different measures of return on sales (ROS). Most other profitability measures relate earnings to a business's assets (mainly equipment and buildings), but since in a design business your biggest and most profitable asset is your design sense (upon which no real, monetary value can be fixed), those types of profitability gauges are not very useful.

For a studio to be viable in the long term it must earn an economic profit, in other words, you must earn a profit over and above the average salary in your area for a senior designer or design manager. If you are only earning a salary and your studio is not earning any additional profit, you must weigh the alternatives to owning your own studio very carefully.

The three profitability measures that you should follow most closely are: 1. Operating profits divided by net sales, 2. Pretax profits divided by net sales, and 3. Net income divided by net sales. The most important is net income—the so-called "bottom line." While your ultimate goal is to maximize this number and to diagnose problems that may be lowering this number, you need to follow the other two measures as well.

If, for example, operating profit divided by net sales is rising but net income over net sales is falling, your studio doesn't have operating problems—it has debt- or tax-related difficulties. If, say, pretax profits divided by net sales is also climbing, you have a tax problem, and you should see your tax adviser to find out if there are any other ways to cut your tax bill. If, on the other hand, pretax profits over sales are falling too, your studio is probably taking on too much debt and interest payments are getting out of hand. If you can pay down your debt without hurting operating profits, you should be able to get your studio's profit picture back on track.

If your studio is generating a net *loss* instead of a net profit, the situation is more serious. If operating profit is negative as well, you need to raise your prices or cut operating costs. However, if operating profit is positive, your problem again may be excessive debt. If depreciation is high, cash flow is probably positive, and you may be able to pay down your debt with cash flow, restoring your studio to profitability. A change in design direction or client type may also cause a short-term dip in profit levels, as will accelerating depreciation on a new asset for tax purposes.

The main point in these examples is that by analyzing your financial statements you and your accountant or business manager should be able to identify major obstacles to greater profitability and, in some cases, find the solutions as well.

A healthy business should have a ratio of net income to net sales of between 3 percent and 7 percent. A ratio of more than 10 percent shows that you are running a very profitable business and that clients will pay a premium for your design expertise. With this in mind, you may consider hiring a production artist or business manager to relieve you of more of the mundane chores in your design studio so that you can further increase profits by devoting more time to design work. (The chart below presents each equation.)

WHAT ABOUT ACCOUNTING SOFTWARE?

For some designers, computerizing accounting chores has made life much easier. For others, the pencil-and-ledger method is still more comfortable. The most important factor in making the decision is whether or not the software program or on-paper accounting system you're trying is easy to use. If it isn't, you may end up spending hundreds of dollars on software or hours and hours setting up a ledger system and then just throwing invoices into a drawer in frustration.

Try out several different software programs on your studio's computer, using real numbers from your current invoices and bills. (Most dealers offer a money-back trial period.) Few design studios require elaborate accounting programs, so don't pay for a lot of extras you probably won't need.

Operating Profit Margin: $\frac{\text{Operating Profit}}{\text{Net Sales}} = \frac{15,000}{194,000} = 7.7\%$

Pretax Profit Margin: $\frac{\text{Pretax Profit}}{\text{Net Sales}} = \frac{14,000}{194,000} = 7.2\%$

Net Profit Margin: $\frac{\text{Net Profit}}{\text{Net Sales}} = \frac{9,100}{194,000} = 4.7\%$

These are the three profitability measures you should follow most closely: the operating profit margin, the pretax profit margin, and your net profit margin. The most important figure is the net profit margin, which is your bottom line. The other two ratios can indicate debt or tax problems that are cutting into your net profit. A ratio of net profit to net sales of 3 to 7 percent is healthy.

PERSONAL PROFILE

BETH MAYNARD
Corey & Co. Designers
New York, New York
Watertown, Massachusetts

"We started out with one IBM personal computer in 1983. We used it to calculate job costs with a system one of our partners, Tom Corey, set up with LOTUS 1-2-3 software," says Beth Maynard, managing partner at Corey & Co. Designers, a design business with an office in New York City and one in Watertown, Massachusetts. "Now we are having a program written for us that integrates a general accounting ledger with a job-costing system. And we're switching to Macintoshes because they have much better capabilities for designers as well as better recordkeeping software."

Maynard and Corey & Co. Designers are not alone in their increasing use of computers to handle recordkeeping and accounting chores. With nine staff members in the New York City office and eleven in Watertown, and a multitude of jobs being handled simultaneously, keeping the books for Corey & Co. Designers is no small task.

"We do a lot of work for entertainment clients, such as the TNT cable channel, Nickelodeon, and other cable television stations. We have several service-oriented clients as well—hospitals, universities. And our design work runs the gamut—from on-air work for our cable clients to brochures, logos, posters and collateral pieces, even annual reports. So for each job, expenses and recordkeeping can be slightly different," says Maynard.

"We considered certain prepackaged job-pricing software systems when we realized we had outgrown the system we had, but most of them were suited more for businesses like architectural design firms rather than graphic designers. By having the program written for us, we wanted to make sure we would have something that would let us grow. We outgrew our other system so quickly that now we want to be sure an accounting/job-pricing system we design can expand as we do," says Maynard.

Under the old accounting system, Corey & Co. needed their accountants to provide monthly income statements so management could keep track of the company's cash flow and financial health. They used the income statements to make business decisions such as whether or not to take on certain jobs or what new equipment or other expansions the company could afford. With the updated system, such numbers will be easily available from any computer terminal, and the company will save accounting costs by requiring only quarterly statements from their accountants rather than the prepared monthly statements they needed before.

"With all of the job files now on computer, time sheet and expense information can be added to the files as soon as it is received, so if a client wants to know how his job is processing, someone can give him up-to-date numbers at the touch of a computer key. This kind of efficiency and accuracy really helps to reassure clients that their money is being well-spent," observes Maynard.

Such recordkeeping also helps to reassure the Internal Revenue Service. In the system, there is a computer listing of the invoices connected with each job, and the actual invoice itself is filed by vendor. Business expenses not billed to a client are filed according to which expense category they belong in.

"It's really the system more than anything that is key. At first hearing, it sounds like a whole lot of bookkeeping. But after you're used to keeping track of costs and time for each job, it becomes almost second nature. Clients know exactly where their money is going, and are reassured that your fees are fair. And pricing a new job becomes much easier. You have complete records of what similar jobs have cost by comparison, and they can help you estimate your costs plus the profit you need on this job to come up with the correct amount to charge for a design. And you can show a prospective client exactly how you came up with your numbers," Maynard says.

Corey & Co. has never been audited. But Maynard feels confident that if they were, the IRS would be satisfied with their recordkeeping. She notes, "When you keep your information simple but thorough, there aren't many holes in it. The whole business runs more smoothly, we can make educated decisions about the firm's expansion, and we can see trouble coming way before it reaches us. And since we're aware of where we stand financially, our designers can feel free to concentrate on what they do best—create and develop terrific designs."

Look for recordkeeping systems that let you assign different expenses to individual projects, yet total the expenses by type as well. Your records will be more informative if you can break them down both by job and by expense category. The former helps you determine the profitability of a given job or jobs, while the latter aids in building financial statements and preparing tax returns.

If your accountant has other designers as clients, or other professionals who create and sell customized products, he or she can give you a good idea of which software program may best meet your needs. You might also want to consider using the same (or compatible) software as your accountant. If records and files you keep can be made available electronically to your accountant, that efficiency will save him time, reduce his fee, and ultimately increase your profits.

FINANCIAL STATUS CHECKLIST

These are the items you should check daily, weekly and monthly to insure your studio's financial health:

Daily

1. Cash on hand.
2. Bank balance.
3. Totals for sales and cash receipts.
4. Records of cash and checks paid out.

Weekly

1. Accounts receivable (Are late payers being pursued?).
2. Accounts payable (Are our bills overdue?).
3. Payroll records (Who was paid how much? Taxes withheld?).
4. Taxes collected and paid (sales, withholding, Social Security).

Monthly

1. Sales and expenses recorded and categorized.
2. Monthly profit-and-loss (or income) statement.
3. Month-end balance sheet.
4. Bank statement (Does it agree with the studio's records?).
5. Petty cash box (Records accurately maintained?).
6. Federal, state and local taxes (Were they paid correctly?).
7. Past-due client bills (Which to continue pursuing and which to write off as losses?).

CHAPTER FOUR
TROUBLESHOOTERS

Q. *My accountant tells me that my studio is making money, and the income statement and balance sheets look good, but cash seems to be awfully low. He explained that this has to do with a computer design system we bought last year. Can you explain?*

A. Your accountant is probably depreciating the cost of the computer design system over several years. Here's how it works: When you depreciate a large purchase, you typically divide the total cost by the number of years you plan to use the equipment, and deduct the same percentage of the total each year. If the equipment cost $20,000 and you planned to depreciate it over five years, you expensed only $4,000 last year and $4,000 this year, but $20,000 has already been spent. So your cash reserve is down $20,000, but only $8,000 has been subtracted from revenues in determining your net profit. This makes sense because you plan to use the equipment over five years, but you need to understand that long-term profitability and short-term liquidity don't necessarily go hand in hand.

Q. *My accountant set up a general ledger for me, but I am very confused by all of the categories it contains for various expense and revenue sources. I find myself plugging in zeros in most of the categories just because I'm not sure what items I should be putting in them. What should I do?*

A. Although it won't distort your financial records to plug in and carry over rows of zeros,

it *is* a waste of your time. Perhaps your accountant didn't understand when he set up the ledger that your studio's finances are fairly clear cut. Work with him to more clearly express your accounting needs and then have him redo the general ledger. The fewer and simpler the categories in your general ledger, the easier it is to keep and the clearer its information is for use in building balance sheets, income statements and cash flow statements.

Q. *I have a one-woman studio for which I handle the bookkeeping chores. When I calculate net income as a percentage of sales, I get huge percentages, often 30 percent to 40 percent profit for the month. My business is doing well, but not spectacularly, so I know these percentages are wrong. What's my mistake?*

A. Most probably, you are forgetting to deduct your implied salary from total sales for the month. Even though you are a sole proprietor, you should calculate an hourly salary for yourself, estimate the number of hours you worked in the month, and deduct your total monthly salary from net sales. The reason this is necessary is because even though you are working for yourself, your time is worth money to your business. Taking your salary into account will give you a more realistic measure of your studio's profit, and a clearer picture of how your studio is really doing.

CHAPTER FOUR
CHECKLISTS

Financial management includes:
- ☐ Managing existing assets and resources profitably.
- ☐ Deciding if and when to take on new assets or staff.
- ☐ Getting loans for new expenditures.
- ☐ Repaying loans with the profits produced by funds previously invested.

Tools used for financial management include:
- ☐ Accounting records.
- ☐ Financial statements.
- ☐ Analysis techniques.

Five basic accounting records you should keep:
- ☐ Sales records.
- ☐ Accounts receivable.
- ☐ Cash receipts.
- ☐ Accounts payable.
- ☐ Cash disbursements.

Financial statements include:
- ☐ General ledger, which records assets, liabilities, owner's equity, revenues, and expenses.
- ☐ Income (profit and loss) statement.
- ☐ Balance sheet.
- ☐ Cash flow statement.

There are two methods of accounting:
- ☐ Cash. This is the simplest method of accounting where you need only keep track of cash revenues and expenses.
- ☐ Accrual. In the accrual method, each revenue item is entered in the ledger as it's incurred, without regard to when actual payment is received or made.

Measure your studio's liquidity by:
- ☐ Calculating your current ratio of assets to liabilities.
- ☐ Figuring out your average collection period.

How to determine whether taking on debt makes good business sense:
- ☐ Determine the cost of the purchase.
- ☐ Calculate the tax savings.
- ☐ Tally the real cost of the purchase.
- ☐ Calculate additional profits the purchase may bring.

Measure your studio's profitability by:
- ☐ Figuring and analyzing your return on sales.
- ☐ Figuring your economic versus your market income.

When you're choosing accounting software:
- ☐ Review your requirements for keeping records.
- ☐ Give the software a trial run with real numbers.
- ☐ Consult an accountant.

Measure your studio's financial status by checking:
- ☐ Daily numbers and records.
- ☐ Weekly numbers and records.
- ☐ Monthly numbers and records.

CHAPTER 5
TAX-SLASHING STRATEGIES

PROFIT POINTS

There are many simple (and legal) ways to pay Uncle Sam less than you did last year by:

- Keeping good records.
- Maximizing your deductions.
- Estimating your taxes correctly to avoid penalties.
- Avoiding audits, or knowing how to deal with them.

Few aspects of a studio's business create more fear and confusion than handling business taxes. Forms and regulations seem to be written in another language, penalties for even accidental underpayment are daunting, and most designers simply rely on their accountants each year.

The good news is that you needn't be a math major to learn how to cut your taxes. There are plenty of simple, legal ways to end up paying Uncle Sam less than you did last year. They consist mostly of keeping better records and knowing about deductions you may have missed in earlier years. This may seem like just more paperwork but keep one thing in mind: Each dollar you save in lower taxes is a dollar more of pure profit for your studio. Not more income, not lower costs, but pure profit. Keeping a lid on your tax bill is one of the best boosts you can give your studio, your career, and your own bank book.

DO YOU NEED A TAX PLANNER?

Unless your tax situation is exceptionally complicated, your accountant should be able to handle your tax planning needs. Complex needs require that you consult a tax attorney with your accountant. The key is to make sure that you hire the right accountant in the first place.

Looking over the books after she has set up a bookkeeping system that you can follow is an important part of what an accountant does for you. But equally important are her tax planning and profit-building strategies for your business. She should be constantly thinking of new ways for your studio to control costs and cut taxes. She should actively analyze where the money is coming in and where it is going out, and how you can work on keeping more of the revenue your studio earns. Since she has an active, working knowledge of your studio's finances, she is the person in the best position to handle your taxes, as long as she shows talent in doing so. That is why the best

idea is to find an accountant who also has tax expertise rather than hiring a separate tax planner or tax attorney whom you only use once a year. (For more on how to choose an accountant, see Chapter Nine.)

HOW TO CALCULATE YOUR TAXES

How much your studio pays in taxes depends on both the amount you earn in a given year and the legal structure of your business.

■ *A sole proprietorship* is a business you run alone that is not incorporated. A standard tax return is filed for such a business just like that of a wage-earner (Form 1040), but the business also files a Schedule C form, which calculates profits or losses from your studio (more on this later).

■ *An unincorporated partnership* is a standard partnership that is not incorporated. The partnership files an information (K1) return, and then each partner files a separate personal tax return reporting as income his share of profits from the business.

■ *A corporation* is a studio of any size (partnership, fifty employees, or just a one-person design firm) that is incorporated. By incorporating a business, you designate your studio as a separate entity from your personal finances for tax and legal purposes. In other words, the corporation employs you, even if you are the only employee it has, and the corporation pays taxes that are entirely separate from your personal income taxes. There can be certain tax and legal advantages to incorporating your studio. Check with your accountant for further details.

■ *A sub-chapter S corporation* is a corporation, but its income is taxed to the shareholders as if it were a partnership. The sub-chapter S corporation option can be a good one because it offers the legal protection of a corporation but allows business losses to offset your personal income.

PERSONAL PROFILE

LARRY W. GOLDSTEIN
Ernst & Young
New York, New York

"One of the biggest tax issues for small design firms these days is the question of whether or not freelancers are technically considered employees or independent contractors," observes Larry W. Goldstein, senior tax manager at the Big Eight accounting firm of Ernst & Young. Goldstein notes that the Internal Revenue Service seems to particularly focus on small businesses (such as one-person studios or partnerships) on this issue, because smaller firms may be more likely to try to avoid the paperwork involved in classifying an on-and-off worker as an employee.

"Basically, the problem runs like this," says Goldstein. "Say you have a small studio with two designers, one production artist, and a business manager/sales representative on staff. During your busy annual report season, you hire a freelance paste-up and mechanicals person to come in three days per week for a month or so to help out your overloaded production artist. The freelancer charges you a daily rate, and at the end of the year you fill out a 1099 listing what you paid her, and send a copy to her and to the IRS. By filing a 1099, you have automatically classified her as an independent contractor, whereas the IRS may rule her to be an employee and penalize you for not having withheld federal taxes from her pay."

Usually both a freelancer and the design studio that hires him or her prefer to classify the work as that of an independent contractor. For the studio, this means very little paperwork—just one form (1099) to be filed at the end of the year with the IRS. And for the freelancer, being paid as an independent contractor means that business deductions may be subtracted from that money, thus making the tax bill lighter. As a self-employed person, an independent contractor is also eligible to set up her own pension plan (Keogh or SEP), and if she loses that self-employed status and becomes an "employee," that plan is taxable just like any investment.

Since IRS rules on who qualifies as an independent contractor have been fairly ambiguous up until recently, both freelancer and employer have chosen to interpret the definition of independent contractor as being fairly broad. But the IRS has decided to change all of that.

"The IRS has now issued a Revenue Ruling (#87-41) that lists all of the aspects of employment that qualify someone as either an employee or independent contractor," notes Goldstein. "Even if you only hire freelancers on rare occasions, you should know the rules of how to handle their fees from a tax standpoint."

According to the IRS, an employee:

- Spends a substantial amount of time working on the premises.
- Works regularly for the same employer.
- Is required to comply with someone else's instructions as to how the work gets done.
- Is trained by the employer.
- Influences the success of the business endeavor with his contribution.
- Must give an employer oral or written progress reports on his work.
- Has business or travel expenses paid by the employer.
- Works with tools and materials provided by the employer.
- Can be terminated by the employer (without cancelling a contract for the work).

Clearly, your best bet is to seek excellent tax and legal advice before setting up or changing the structure of your studio. A good tax or small business attorney can look at your current tax payments, other sources of income, and your personal finances and decide which type of legal set-up is best for your studio. Trust her judgment, but, as always, make sure you fully understand *why* a certain legal structure was chosen and what the drawbacks may be if the studio's business changes a great deal or tax laws are modified.

WHICH TAXES YOUR STUDIO MUST PAY

- *Federal income tax estimates and withholding.* As a sole proprietor or partner, you

An independent contractor, according to the IRS:

- Maintains a separate office or work-space from the employer.
- Can realize a profit or loss on a job, rather than just receiving a salary.
- Works for more than one employer.
- Advertises or makes available his services to the general public.
- Hires, supervises and pays his own assistant.

"The problem is, of course, that many freelancers, especially in the design field, meet some of the criteria for each category. If you are unsure about how to handle a freelancer's tax status, ask his or her preference, check with your accountant/tax advisor, and review the IRS rules. You may decide simply to handle the paperwork for each freelancer as if he or she were an employee, to be on the safe side," says Goldstein.

Hiring a company like ADP, which handles payroll systems, may not be a bad idea if you really detest all of the paperwork. Each employee must fill out a W-4 form to determine how much federal tax should be withheld, and then at year's end your studio sends the IRS and each employee a W-2 form that totals his or her wages for the year.

If you want to avoid claiming freelancers as employees, then you may want to modify the ways in which you use their services in order to meet the independent contractor guidelines. If possible, let freelancers work on the project more independently, use their own studio space and materials (you can include their cost in the freelancer's fee), and pay them a flat fee per project, not a daily or hourly rate.

are required by law to pay federal income tax on the income you receive *as you earn it*. This means you must pay quarterly estimated taxes (usually due on the 15th of the months of January, April, June and September). In April of each year, you are required to file Form 1040ES, which contains a worksheet for estimating the next year's income.

If your studio is incorporated, you are liable for filing and paying corporate income tax. There are two major tax issues specific to corporations you should be aware of. First of all, you can elect to adopt your own fiscal year of operation, for example April 1 to March 31 of the next year instead of the traditional January 1 to December 31. Your accountant or attorney can tell you about the tax advantages of an alternate year-end.

Second, although your salary is considered a deductible expense when calculating your pretax corporate income, you are still responsible for paying personal income taxes on your salary. Since your salary (and dividends, if any) is drawn from your corporate income, many people feel that they are being double-taxed in this situation.

Corporate income taxes tend to be complex and should be handled by your accountant or a tax specialist.

If you have any employees, you are also required to withhold federal and state income taxes for them, and to supply them and the federal government with Form W-2 at the end of the year listing their wages and taxes withheld. If you hire freelancers or independent contractors, you must file a Form 1099 with the federal government (and send a copy to them) that tells how much you paid each one.

- *Social Security self-employment tax.* All companies must withhold Social Security taxes from their employees' wages, then match the amount withheld and send the total to the IRS on a quarterly basis. If you are a sole proprietor or self-employed partner, you must pay both amounts, since you are both the employee and the employer in this case. The amount of tax you owe is calculated on Form 1040SE.

- *Unemployment tax.* If you have paid wages of at least $1,500 to employee(s) in a quarter or employed someone at least one day in each of twenty or more calendar weeks, you must pay unemployment tax. Unemployment tax payments must be deposited in an authorized commercial or Federal Reserve Bank using Form 508. An annual return for unemployment tax must be filed with the IRS using Form 940 by January 31 after the year for which the tax has been calculated.

■ *State and local taxes.* Tax laws vary a great deal from state to state. Every state has a state unemployment tax, and many have income and sales taxes. Counties, cities and towns also impose different kinds of taxes, so it is especially important that you find an accountant/tax advisor who has worked locally for a number of years and understands the workings of all tax laws in the geographic area where you are doing business.

RECORDKEEPING

One of the things a financially responsible design studio needs is a coherent, workable, up-to-date recordkeeping system. You need to keep a record of your studio's income and expenditures for three reasons: to document tax deductions and provide a record of taxable income, to keep a finger on the financial pulse of your studio, and to help determine if you are charging rates for jobs that include a fair profit for your business. While each of these is a compelling reason to keep accurate records, backing up your tax returns and documenting deductions is one of the most important.

The Internal Revenue Service (IRS) puts the burden of proof on the taxpayer when he or she files a tax return. In other words, instead of being innocent until proven guilty (as in the American legal system), taxpayers are assumed to have no legitimate tax deductions unless they can provide proof that such deductions are valid. An effective recordkeeping system does just that.

You should keep records of all income and all expenses for your studio. Any money that comes in or goes out should be recorded. It's not even that important to know whether or not certain expenses are deductible (although spending studio dollars on deductible expenses will lower your pretax income and reduce your taxes). What is important is that you keep track of all money that is spent for your business and what it is spent on, and that your

accountant sort out which expenditures are deductible against business income. The key point is that you keep accurate, accessible and standardized records. If the IRS sees no proof that the money was spent on a legitimate deduction, then for their purposes it never was, and those lost tax deductions come directly out of your studio's profits.

You will find it much easier to keep accurate records by starting a separate job file for each commissioned work. You should keep two files, one containing the different sketches and paste-ups that show how the design was created, and a second file to hold receipts, time sheets, client correspondence, meeting notes, etc., for the job. Such a file system makes it easier to find the right records when you need them at tax time, and can be used to show clients exactly how you created the design they are paying for.

If at all possible, segregate your business records from your personal finances, even if you work from a studio in your home. For example, you should have separate bank accounts for your studio and your personal monies, and you should put in a different telephone line for business calls if you have a home studio. If your studio has a name different from your own (e.g., "Phoebe Jones Designs" rather than just "Phoebe Jones"), be sure that checks are made payable to your studio, not you, so there is no confusion as to what is and isn't business income. If you take out a business loan for new equipment or other expansion, you'll need to prove that the money was never used for personal expenditures in order for the interest payments to be deductible, and that is much harder to do when your studio's money and your own are kept in a single account.

You'll also have an easier time proving business deductions if you pay all suppliers' bills with checks from your business account. The cancelled check generally provides an adequate record for a tax deduction.

Get into the habit of asking for a receipt whenever you make any kind of business expenditure. Even small purchases like a single stat or taxi ride should be documented whenever possible for reimbursement from petty cash as well as eventual deduction from the year's business income.

What you should keep:

- Invoices and monthly statements.
- Receipts.
- Cancelled checks.
- Bank statements.
- Corporate credit card statements.
- Contracts.
- Letters confirming verbal agreements or changes in a contract.
- Bank deposit and withdrawal slips.
- Monthly utility bills.

You should also keep a daily log or journal to note incidental expenses for which you have no receipts (e.g., tips to a taxi driver or public transportation costs) and to document the everyday running of your studio. Many people simply incorporate such a journal into their daily appointments calendar, noting any smaller, "receipt-less" expenses on the day they were incurred. Save the book as a record of your business year. In several cases, the IRS has accepted a full year's deduction for items that were noted for only part of the year simply because the documentation for those parts of the year was so thorough that they felt it could be extrapolated for the entire year. However, keep in mind that such an expense log should only be used to note smaller amounts for which you have no receipt.

One area of recordkeeping that designers often overlook is automobile usage. If you use your own car for business purposes (e.g., driving to meet clients, traveling to visit and compare suppliers) you may deduct a percentage of the maintenance costs and the gas consumed. Keep a log book in the car's glove compartment, and note the date, odometer readings before and after the trip, miles driven, and purpose of each business trip.

Besides the expenses log discussed above, you should keep a business checkbook that provides plenty of room on the stub for explanations of what checks cover, including invoice or account numbers. When a cancelled check is not enough proof for the IRS to allow a deduction, a detailed account of what the check covered and, if available, an invoice requesting the payment most often are acceptable backup.

It's also a good idea to keep a book of petty cash vouchers with which to record small cash expenditures. These vouchers also help you to get proper reimbursement from your business when you use your own money to temporarily cover small expenses.

The last kind of book you may need for recordkeeping is a payroll journal, if you have employees on staff. Use it to record gross salary, taxes withheld, social security withheld, etc. Even if you only hire freelancers, you should keep a separate file for each, documenting whom you've paid, how much, and for what (using their invoice to you as a basis for payment). You need to file a 1099 form with the IRS at the end of the year listing payments to independent contractors.

Organizing Your Receipts

It is important to keep your receipts in an orderly fashion. It is much easier for your accountant to sort through your records and find the deductions you deserve if your receipts are organized and categorized. All vendors and suppliers should have their own file folder in your filing system. You should mark each invoice with the word "PAID," the date, the amount paid, and the number of the check used. This should be done at the time payment is made.

Try filing miscellaneous and small, one-time receipts in a series of file folders or envelopes, one for each of the different deduction categories on the Schedule C form (see detailed categories later on in this chapter). Your accountant can help you understand those categories when you set up the sorting system. When you come across a receipt for an expenditure that you're not sure can be deducted, or for which you don't know the category, put it in a separate folder for "I don't know's." Later,

PERSONAL PROFILE

REID GUNTER
Hamilton, Cleveland & Grey
Charlotte, North Carolina

We all know we should keep better tax records, but few of us make the effort. Here's a horror story, however, that may help convince you of the value of keeping good records for your studio the way no amount of reminding will.

"The letter arrived on my desk during my second week at Hamilton, Cleveland & Grey," says Reid Gunter, business manager for the Charlotte, North Carolina-based design firm. "It was a fairly strongly worded statement from the Internal Revenue Service informing us that if we did not send in our long-overdue withholding taxes shortly, there would be a lien placed on our business property to help ensure proper payment of our tax bill. You can be sure I was worried."

Hamilton, Cleveland & Grey is not the kind of company that is in the habit of being chased by creditors. Founded by partners Patrick Elam and Tom Puckett (who met while working on *Savannah* magazine), the five-person design firm has grown into one of the hottest new design studios in the Southeast. Although their initial focus was mostly graphics for small companies (annual reports, logos, direct mail pieces, and collaterals), they are in the process of changing design direction, doing more media placement work and targeting larger clients for national campaigns. Currently, they handle clients from all over the country. Dixon Ticonderoga, Flowers Industries, American Efrid, Raycom Sports Management, Kitchen Capers, and GITA Sporting Goods are just a few of the companies Hamilton, Cleveland & Grey have worked with over the past few years.

Gunter continues: "The first thing I did was go to our records. I found that, according to our information, withholding taxes had been paid promptly and in full. So I got on the telephone—and *stayed* on the telephone."

According to Gunter, trying to get through to the correct problems resolution person at the regional office was almost as nerve-racking as receiving the underpayment notices and being threatened with legal action. After weeks of either being unable to get through on the toll-free number provided, or actually making contact but then being put on hold for 15 minutes or longer, Gunter finally got reassurance that the Hamilton, Cleveland & Grey account was in good standing and that he needn't worry further about the erroneous letters.

But at the same time that one part of the IRS was assuring Gunter that all was well, another division continued to hound Hamilton, Cleveland & Grey for supposed non-payment of employee withholding taxes. When the whole mess was finally straightened out, the last letter Gunter received was an apology from the regional director of the Internal Revenue Service office in Memphis, Tennessee.

What happened is the IRS had three different tax identification account numbers for Hamilton, Cleveland & Grey. The company first started out as a limited partnership, and at that time it received a tax identification number. Then, when it became an S corporation and the structure in which it paid taxes changed, it received a new tax identification number. Not too long after that, the company was incorporated, and as a separate tax entity, it was given yet a third corporate tax account number. The problem was that the earlier numbers should have been superseded, but no one took care of it. So while Hamilton, Cleveland & Grey, the corporation, was happily passing on its employee withholding each quarter and being credited correctly for those amounts, Hamilton, Cleveland & Grey the limited partnership had suddenly stopped paying its withholding taxes. "That was because the company as a limited partnership did not exist anymore, but it took the IRS a lot of investigation to finally figure that out and remedy the situation," says Gunter. "Thank goodness we had the records of tax payments made to back up our case, or I'm sure we'd still be in the middle of this dispute."

The IRS sent Gunter a new booklet that is marked with the current tax identification number and asked him to start making payments from that booklet. Even they are tired of trying to straighten out the mess—they asked Hamilton, Cleveland & Grey to start making tax payments at the next due date and plan to wipe out all of the old account numbers and start from scratch.

What about that letter of apology? "I plan to frame it and hang it over my desk," says Gunter. "It's not often that Goliath apologizes to David, you know. And there is a lesson to be learned from this: Keeping good records kept us from being hurt by *their* mistake."

your accountant will advise you on the correct category.

Often the best receipt for a business expense is a charge slip. Most slips now have forms printed on the back, which you can fill in with details about the nature of the expenditure (purpose, persons entertained, date, amount, place, etc.) Even if no preprinting is on the back of your receipt, write the information anyway. If accurately documented, these detailed charge slips can help your deduction stand up under possible IRS scrutiny. Keeping receipts is easy if you set up a corporate charge account. Most corporate charge cards now provide an itemized year-end statement that divides charges into deduction categories, helping to make tax return preparation much more convenient.

If your studio is computerized, you might try one of the expense-tracking software programs now available. These programs prompt you to put in all of the details required for IRS deductibility, and keep track of daily and weekly totals in each deduction category for you. You should be able to try out several programs at your local software dealer and pick the one best suited for your needs, or consult your accountant for a recommendation and possible compatibility with his or her system.

TAKE THE GUESSWORK OUT OF ESTIMATED TAXES

You must pay estimated federal taxes on income earned by freelancing or being self-employed. Estimated taxes are paid on a quarterly basis, and most people fill out a 1040ES form in April to estimate what they believe they will earn over the next year. If you don't want to be subject to an underpayment penalty, you must prepay at least 90 percent of your tax liability, either through withholding or estimated tax payments. The one exception to this rule is that you need to prepay only 100 percent of your *last year's* tax liability. So, if you owed much less in taxes last year than you will this year, you could get away with prepaying under 90 percent of this year's liability without incurring the underpayment penalty. Some states

also require estimated payment of state and local taxes. Your accountant or tax planner should help you calculate estimated tax payments and remind you to make them when they are due.

HOW TO MAXIMIZE YOUR DEDUCTIONS

A Schedule C (Profit or Loss From Business or Profession) is filed with your 1040 federal tax return on April 15. Most state tax forms also require that you include a copy of the Schedule C from your federal return. Sole proprietorships and sub chapter S corporations use this form to report all studio income and claim all business deductions. Since the amount of tax you owe is computed using the amount of profit you declare on your Schedule C (gross income minus business deductions), it is in your studio's best interests that you make sure every deductible expense is declared.

Part I of the Schedule C is used to total your business's gross income (gross receipts minus the cost of the goods the business has sold). Since most design businesses don't purchase inventories of goods and then resell them, typically a studio's gross receipts approximate or equal its gross income. Therefore, Part III (Cost of Goods Sold and/or Operations) is left blank.

Part II is for itemizing the expenses you can deduct from gross income. Again, remember that any deduction you claim here must be backed up with a receipt and explanation of exactly what the money was spent for. Also, keep in mind that deductions must be of a reasonable amount for the category. For example, $10,000 is very little to spend on advertising and promotion for a studio that bills $300,000 a year, but it's way too much for a one-person operation that billed only $47,000 last year. If for some valid reason a deduction amount is higher than may seem reasonable, attach an explanation to the Schedule C detailing what the money was spent for and why. It's better to dispel doubts on the return itself than to risk being called in for an audit.

Following is a list of the deduction categories most relevant to a design studio and what kinds of expenses fall under each:

■ *Advertising.* Include items such as the costs of promotional brochures, resumes, stationery, business cards, media ads, and any fees paid to marketing consultants.

■ *Bad debts.* These are a sad fact of doing business, so make sure you get the proper deduction if someone stiffs you. The bad debt is only deductible, however, if you have previously calculated it as income and if you are using the cash method of accounting. (See Chapter Four for an explanation of accounting methods.)

■ *Bank service charges.* Total all monthly surcharges, automatic-teller machine, per-check and bounced-check charges your studio paid on its account.

■ *Car and truck expenses.* This is a sticky area that often comes under IRS scrutiny, so be sure to keep an accurate mileage log to document how much you used your car for business. Also note in the logbook the total mileage each January 1, so you'll know how many miles you drove last year, and what percentage of those total miles were for business. You may deduct that percentage of all of the costs related to operating the car. Some taxpayers, however, prefer to take a standard mileage rate deduction instead. Last year's flat rate was 26 cents per mile up to 15,000 miles, and 11 cents after that. Check with your accountant for his advice on whether to use the flat rate or your own percentage — once you use one method with a car you cannot change to the other deduction method in following tax years.

■ *Commissions.* If any of your work is handled by an agent or gallery, deduct their commissions here.

■ *Depreciation.* In general, it is to your advantage to deduct the total amount of any equipment purchase in the year in which you bought it. However, there are certain types of equipment that must be depreciated (deducted in parts over several years rather than in one lump deduction). Your accountant should be able to counsel you on which kinds of equipment fall into this category and which

method of depreciation will be most significant in maximizing your studio's profits.

If you own a home and have studio space in it, or if you own studio space elsewhere, the business's asset must be depreciated. This is a complicated procedure best handled by your accountant.

■ *Dues and publications.* Deduct the costs of any art or design books you bought over the year, subscription costs for all art and design journals, and dues paid to any professional group or guild, such as the Graphic Artists Guild or Artists in Print.

■ *Insurance.* Besides the standard business insurance costs for protection against fire, theft and liability, make sure to deduct the costs of any special insurance for your studio, such as documents-in-transit insurance or valuable-papers coverage.

■ *Legal and professional services.* This category can also provide a substantial deduction for most design studios. Total all of the fees you paid accountants, attorneys and other consultants.

■ *Office expense.* Total the costs of office supplies, postage and similar expenses and deduct them here.

■ *Rental or lease of machinery, equipment or other business property.* A small studio often leases a copier, stat camera or even furniture, the rent for all of which should be deducted against gross income. If you rent office space, you should deduct the cost on this line as well.

■ *Taxes.* You can deduct real estate and personal property taxes on business assets, social security taxes paid to match withholding from your employee's wages, federal unemployment taxes paid, and federal highway use tax. But do *not* deduct federal income, gift, estate, property, or state and local sales taxes.

For the self-employed taxpayer, Schedule C (pages 73-74) can be the most important schedule in your return. Schedule C is where you will report your self-employment income and claim your business deductions.

SCHEDULE C
(Form 1040)

Department of the Treasury
Internal Revenue Service   (0)

Profit or Loss From Business
(Sole Proprietorship)
Partnerships, Joint Ventures, Etc., Must File Form 1065.
▶ **Attach to Form 1040 or Form 1041.**   ▶ **See Instructions for Schedule C (Form 1040).**

OMB No. 1545-0074

19**90**

Attachment
Sequence No. **09**

Name of proprietor: *Terry Cotta*

Social security number (SSN)

A Principal business or profession, including product or service (see Instructions)   *Designer*

B Enter principal business code
(from page 2) ▶ | 8 | 8 | 8 | 8 |

C Business name and address ▶ (include suite or room no.)   *11275 Littleton Rd., Cincinnati OH 45267*

D Employer ID number (Not SSN)

E Accounting method: (1) ☒ Cash   (2) ☐ Accrual   (3) ☐ Other (specify) ▶ ....

F Method(s) used to value closing inventory: (1) ☒ Cost   (2) ☐ Lower of cost or market   (3) ☐ Other (attach explanation)   (4) ☐ Does not apply (if checked, go to line H)

		Yes	No
G	Was there any change in determining quantities, costs, or valuations between opening and closing inventory? (If "Yes," attach explanation.)		✕
H	Are you deducting expenses for business use of your home? (If "Yes," see Instructions for limitations.)	✕	
I	Did you "materially participate" in the operation of this business during 1990? (If "No," see Instructions for limitations on losses.)	✕	
J	If this is the first Schedule C filed for this business, check here ▶ ☐		

Part I   Income

1	Gross receipts or sales. *Caution: If this income was reported to you on Form W-2 and the "Statutory employee" box on that form was checked, see the Instructions and check here* ▶ ☐	**1**	11000
2	Returns and allowances	**2**	
3	Subtract line 2 from line 1. Enter the result here	**3**	11000
4	Cost of goods sold (from line 38 on page 2)	**4**	
5	Subtract line 4 from line 3 and enter the **gross profit** here	**5**	11000
6	Other income, including Federal and state gasoline or fuel tax credit or refund (see Instructions)	**6**	
7	Add lines 5 and 6. This is your **gross income** ▶	**7**	11000

Part II   Expenses

8	Advertising	**8**	50	21	Repairs and maintenance	**21**	
9	Bad debts from sales or services (see Instructions)	**9**		22	Supplies (not included in Part III)	**22**	250
10	Car and truck expenses (attach **Form 4562**)	**10**	150	23	Taxes and licenses	**23**	
11	Commissions and fees	**11**		24	Travel, meals, and entertainment:		
12	Depletion	**12**		**a**	Travel	**24a**	150
13	Depreciation and section 179 expense deduction (not included in Part III) (see Instructions)	**13**		**b**	Meals and entertainment		
				c	Enter 20% of line 24b subject to limitations (see Instructions)		
14	Employee benefit programs (other than on line 19)	**14**		**d**	Subtract line 24c from line 24b	**24d**	
15	Insurance (other than health)	**15**	100	25	Utilities	**25**	
16	Interest:			26	Wages (less jobs credit)	**26**	
a	Mortgage (paid to banks, etc.)	**16a**		27a	Other expenses (**list type and amount**):		
b	Other	**16b**			....		
17	Legal and professional services	**17**	250		....		
18	Office expense	**18**	50		....		
19	Pension and profit-sharing plans	**19**			....		
20	Rent or lease (see Instructions):				....		
a	Vehicles, machinery, and equip.	**20a**					
b	Other business property	**20b**		27b	Total other expenses	**27b**	

28	Add amounts in columns for lines 8 through 27b. These are your **total expenses** ▶	**28**	1000
29	**Net profit or (loss).** Subtract line 28 from line 7. If a profit, enter here and on Form 1040, line 12. Also enter the net profit on Schedule SE, line 2 (statutory employees, see Instructions). If a loss, you MUST go on to line 30 (fiduciaries, see Instructions)	**29**	10000

30 If you have a loss, you MUST check the box that describes your investment in this activity (see Instructions).
If you checked 30a, enter the loss on Form 1040, line 12, and Schedule SE, line 2 (statutory employees, see Instructions). If you checked 30b, you MUST attach **Form 6198**.

30a ☐ All investment is at risk.
30b ☐ Some investment is not at risk.

For Paperwork Reduction Act Notice, see Form 1040 Instructions.

Schedule C (Form 1040) 1990

Schedule C (Form 1040) 1990 — Page **2**

Part III Cost of Goods Sold (See Instructions.)

31 Inventory at beginning of year. (If different from last year's closing inventory, attach explanation.)	**31**	
32 Purchases less cost of items withdrawn for personal use	**32**	
33 Cost of labor. (Do not include salary paid to yourself.)	**33**	
34 Materials and supplies	**34**	
35 Other costs	**35**	
36 Add lines 31 through 35	**36**	
37 Inventory at end of year	**37**	
38 **Cost of goods sold.** Subtract line 37 from line 36. Enter the result here and on page 1, line 4	**38**	

Part IV Principal Business or Professional Activity Codes

Locate the major category that best describes your activity. Within the major category, select the activity code that most closely identifies the business or profession that is the principal source of your sales or receipts. **Enter this 4-digit code on page 1, line B.** *For example, a grocery store is under the major category of "Retail Trade," and the code is "3210."* **(Note:** *If your principal source of income is from farming activities, you should file* **Schedule F (Form** *1040), Farm Income and Expenses.)*

Construction

Code
0018 Operative builders (for own account)

General contractors
0034 Residential building
0059 Nonresidential building
0075 Highway and street construction
3889 Other heavy construction (pipe laying, bridge construction, etc.)

Building trade contractors, including repairs
0232 Plumbing, heating, air conditioning
0257 Painting and paper hanging
0273 Electrical work
0299 Masonry, dry wall, stone, tile
0414 Carpentering and flooring
0430 Roofing, siding, and sheet metal
0455 Concrete work
0885 Other building trade contractors (excavation, glazing, etc.)

Manufacturing, Including Printing and Publishing
0638 Food products and beverages
0653 Textile mill products
0679 Apparel and other textile products
0695 Leather, footware, handbags, etc.
0810 Furniture and fixtures
0836 Lumber and other wood products
0851 Printing and publishing
0877 Paper and allied products
1032 Stone, clay, and glass products
1057 Primary metal industries
1073 Fabricated metal products
1099 Machinery and machine shops
1115 Electric and electronic equipment
1883 Other manufacturing industries

Mining and Mineral Extraction
1511 Metal mining
1537 Coal mining
1552 Oil and gas
1719 Quarrying and nonmetallic mining

Agricultural Services, Forestry, Fishing
1933 Crop services
1958 Veterinary services, including pets
1974 Livestock breeding
1990 Other animal services
2113 Farm labor and management services
2212 Horticulture and landscaping
2238 Forestry, except logging
0836 Logging
2246 Commercial fishing
2469 Hunting and trapping

Wholesale Trade—Selling Goods to Other Businesses, Etc.

Durable goods, including machinery, equipment, wood, metals, etc.
2618 Selling for your own account
2634 Agent or broker for other firms— more than 50% of gross sales on commission

Nondurable goods, including food, fiber, chemicals, etc.
2659 Selling for your own account

2675 Agent or broker for other firms— more than 50% of gross sales on commission

Retail Trade—Selling Goods to Individuals and Households
3012 Selling door-to-door, by telephone or party plan, or from mobile unit
3038 Catalog or mail order
3053 Vending machine selling

Selling From Showroom, Store, or Other Fixed Location

Food, beverages, and drugs
3079 Eating places (meals or snacks)
3086 Catering services
3095 Drinking places (alcoholic beverages)
3210 Grocery stores (general line)
0612 Bakeries selling at retail
3236 Other food stores (meat, produce, candy, etc.)
3251 Liquor stores
3277 Drug stores

Automotive and service stations
3319 New car dealers (franchised)
3335 Used car dealers
3517 Other automotive dealers (motorcycles, recreational vehicles, etc.)
3533 Tires, accessories, and parts
3558 Gasoline service stations

General merchandise, apparel, and furniture
3715 Variety stores
3731 Other general merchandise stores
3756 Shoe stores
3772 Men's and boys' clothing stores
3913 Women's ready-to-wear stores
3921 Women's accessory and specialty stores and furriers
3939 Family clothing stores
3954 Other apparel and accessory stores
3970 Furniture stores
3996 TV, audio, and electronics
3988 Computer and software stores
4119 Household appliance stores
4317 Other home furnishing stores (china, floor coverings, etc.)
4333 Music and record stores

Building, hardware, and garden supply
4416 Building materials dealers
4432 Paint, glass, and wallpaper stores
4457 Hardware stores
4473 Nurseries and garden supply stores

Other retail stores
4614 Used merchandise and antique stores (except motor vehicle parts)
4630 Gift, novelty, and souvenir shops
4655 Florists
4671 Jewelry stores
4697 Sporting goods and bicycle shops
4812 Boat dealers
4838 Hobby, toy, and game shops
4853 Camera and photo supply stores
4879 Optical goods stores
4895 Luggage and leather goods stores
5017 Book stores, excluding newsstands
5033 Stationery stores
5058 Fabric and needlework stores
5074 Mobile home dealers
5090 Fuel dealers (except gasoline)
5884 Other retail stores

Finance, Insurance, Real Estate, and Related Services
5520 Real estate agents or brokers
5579 Real estate property managers
5710 Subdividers and developers, except cemeteries
5538 Operators and lessors of buildings, including residential
5553 Operators and lessors of other real property
5702 Insurance agents or brokers
5744 Other insurance services
6064 Security brokers and dealers
6080 Commodity contracts brokers and dealers, and security and commodity exchanges
6130 Investment advisors and services
6148 Credit institutions and mortgage bankers
6155 Title abstract offices
5777 Other finance and real estate

Transportation, Communications, Public Utilities, and Related Services
6114 Taxicabs
6312 Bus and limousine transportation
6361 Other highway passenger transportation
6338 Trucking (except trash collection)
6395 Courier or package delivery services
6510 Trash collection without own dump
6536 Public warehousing
6551 Water transportation
6619 Air transportation
6635 Travel agents and tour operators
6650 Other transportation services
6676 Communication services
6692 Utilities, including dumps, snowplowing, road cleaning, etc.

Services (Personal, Professional, and Business Services)

Hotels and other lodging places
7096 Hotels, motels, and tourist homes
7211 Rooming and boarding houses
7237 Camps and camping parks

Laundry and cleaning services
7419 Coin-operated laundries and dry cleaning
7435 Other laundry, dry cleaning, and garment services
7450 Carpet and upholstery cleaning
7476 Janitorial and related services (building, house, and window cleaning)

Business and/or personal services
7617 Legal services (or lawyer)
7633 Income tax preparation
7658 Accounting and bookkeeping
7518 Engineering services
7682 Architectural services
7708 Surveying services
7245 Management services
7260 Public relations
7286 Consulting services
7716 Advertising, except direct mail
7732 Employment agencies and personnel supply
7799 Consumer credit reporting and collection services

7856 Mailing, reproduction, commercial art and photography, and stenographic services
7872 Computer programming, processing, data preparation, and related services
7922 Computer repair, maintenance, and leasing
7773 Equipment rental and leasing (except computer or automotive)
7914 Investigative and protective services
7880 Other business services

Personal services
8110 Beauty shops (or beautician)
8318 Barber shop (or barber)
8334 Photographic portrait studios
8532 Funeral services and crematories
8714 Child day care
8730 Teaching or tutoring
8755 Counseling (except health practitioners)
8771 Ministers and chaplains
6882 Other personal services

Automotive services
8813 Automotive rental or leasing, without driver
8839 Parking, except valet
8953 Automotive repairs, general and specialized
8896 Other automotive services (wash, towing, etc.)

Miscellaneous repair, except computers
9019 TV and audio equipment repair
9035 Other electrical equipment repair
9050 Reupholstery and furniture repair
2881 Other equipment repair

Medical and health services
9217 Offices and clinics of medical doctors (MDs)
9233 Offices and clinics of dentists
9258 Osteopathic physicians and surgeons
9241 Podiatrists
9274 Chiropractors
9290 Optometrists
9415 Registered and practical nurses
9431 Other health practitioners
9456 Medical and dental laboratories
9472 Nursing and personal care facilities
9886 Other health services

Amusement and recreational services
8557 Physical fitness facilities
9597 Motion picture and video production
9688 Motion picture and tape distribution and allied services
9613 Videotape rental
9639 Motion picture theaters
9670 Bowling centers
9696 Professional sports and racing, including promoters and managers
9811 Theatrical performers, musicians, agents, producers, and related services
9837 Other amusement and recreational services

8888 Unable to classify

*U.S. GPO: 1990-265-185

■ *Travel, meals and entertainment.* This is another deduction area that the IRS pays special attention to. A receipt for business travel must include the time and date, place and purpose of the business trip, plus the amount spent. Besides the information required for travel deductions, an entertainment or meal receipt must also list the people entertained and their business relationship to your studio (for example, a partner or potential client). Travel expenses, as long as they are exclusively for business and not deemed "exorbitant" by the IRS, are 100 percent deductible, but you can only take 80 percent of your meals and entertainment tabs as a deduction.

■ *Utilities.* Deductions should be fairly clear cut here, unless you have a home studio. The IRS has now disallowed deducting the base rate for a home telephone that you also use for business. When you figure what percentage of your square footage is used for business purposes (see below under Home Office Deductions), deduct that same percentage of heat, gas, water and electricity bills on this line.

■ *Other expenses.* Don't feel like certain expenses aren't deductible simply because the Schedule C doesn't list a category for them. List any other expenses here, with a brief description. Some designers use this space to list a home studio deduction as well.

The above list was designed to give you general hints about making the most of your studio's deductions. A skilled accountant, however, will be able to provide more specific advice on how your business can maximize its allowable deductions.

DEDUCTING A HOME STUDIO

This can be a tricky set of deductions to back up, but it is usually well worth the effort. Be forewarned, however, that checking the "Yes" box for the question "Are you claiming a home office deduction?" on your Schedule C automatically makes the IRS take a closer look at your return, and increases your chances for an IRS audit. Make sure your home studio deduction is legitimate in the IRS's eyes and can be solidly backed up with records and receipts.

In order for the expenses related to your studio space (usually rent or mortgage principal and maintenance payments) to be allowed as a business deduction, the space must meet certain IRS requirements. They are as follows:

■ *Exclusive use.* You must be able to prove that your studio space and the equipment in it are used *exclusively* for business purposes. The space may be used for no other purpose; therefore, it shouldn't contain things such as a television or fold-out couch that may show another use.

■ *Regular and principal place of business.* Besides being used only for business, the studio must be the *primary* place in which you design, and you must have been using it *continually* and *frequently* to create designs.

Once you have met the above requirements, you must determine what percentage of your home the studio space occupies. The easiest way to do this is to use square footage. For instance, if your home is 1,800 square feet total and your studio measures 270 square feet, then you are using 15 percent (270 divided by 1,800) of your living space as a studio. Thus you may deduct 15 percent of the total you pay in rent or on a mortgage and maintenance, and 15 percent of utilities. You may not, however, take a home office deduction that exceeds your studio's gross income. In this case, other IRS rules apply; talk with your accountant about how to deduct home office expenses when you have a net business loss.

AUDITS

On a percentage basis, your chances of being selected for an IRS audit are slim. However, with the advent of computer processing, it is likely that at some point in your studio's lifespan, your business tax return will be at least casually questioned.

Before we discuss how to survive an audit, it's worth mentioning some techniques to make one less likely.

■ *Don't take questionable deductions.* For instance, in a business like design a $3,000 deduction for studio rent makes a lot more sense than a $3,000 deduction for laundry and cleaning.

■ *Don't use the wrong tax preparer.* Believe it or not, the IRS watches certain accountants who have prepared a higher-than-normal number of returns that have been questioned or audited. When you interview accountants and tax preparers, be sure to ask which of their recent clients have been audited and why.

■ *Don't round off numbers.* An even $300 deduction for postage costs sounds more like a rough estimate than an accurate, documented total. Numbers should be rounded only to the nearest whole dollar.

■ *Don't take single, huge deductions without complete and accurate documentation.* Even if your studio billed $275,000 last year, a single deduction of, say, $40,000 may appear suspect.

■ *Don't be sloppy.* Sometimes mere bad handwriting or improperly added numbers act as a red flag for an audit.

The Taxpayer Bill of Rights provides taxpayers with certain protections in facing an IRS audit. It states that you must be informed of your rights at all times when dealing with an IRS agent, that you may send a qualified accountant, tax preparer or other representative to handle the audit for you in most cases, that you may make an audio recording of the audit proceedings, and that you have the right to have the audit conducted at a time and place convenient for you. Best of all, the new legislation states that the IRS may no longer evaluate its auditors based on how much revenue they bring in. In other words, IRS agents now are promoted for reaching equitable solutions in audits, not for milking taxpayers for every penny they can get.

There are four kinds of tax audits:

■ *Correspondence audit.* The IRS simply wants to see the documentation for certain items. Send back the cancelled check or receipt that backs up each item, but make copies in case they get lost in the mail or at the IRS office.

■ *Office audit.* You are asked to come into the local IRS office to answer questions about your return. Bring your tax preparer or other representative with you, and record the proceedings. Be sure to get *in writing* a list of the specific items on the return that the IRS agent would like to discuss and see documentation for. Bring only that documentation. Don't start discussing items that were not questioned in writing—you may open up whole new areas of investigation. If a request for an office audit is purposely vague, ask for further details about which items are being questioned before setting up a time to meet with an IRS agent.

■ *Field examination audit.* Self-employed people with small businesses or home work space are often targeted for this kind of audit. Agents want to see if your lifestyle is commensurate with the amount of income you are claiming, and if your home studio meets exclusive-use requirements. They may also visit your place of business if it is not at your home. But the same protections apply as under an office audit. Ask that they detail what they will be examining when they come to visit, and show them only what they have previously asked for.

■ *Taxpayer compliance measurement program audit.* The IRS picks a very small number of returns at random for microscopic inspection. If you have been selected, it doesn't automatically mean you are at fault or guilty of a tax violation. Make sure your records are accurate and coherent.

In general, it is to the IRS's advantage to settle any tax dispute quickly and reasonably. While you want to be cooperative, don't be intimidated by a tough-talking auditor. Don't be afraid to bargain. For example, you should be able to get reduced penalties on some items if you give up other deductions for which documentation is less than complete. Also, negotiate a payment schedule that you can live with. And consider hiring a tax representative—his or her expertise may save you plenty of penalties, interest, back taxes, time, and emotional wear and tear, especially if your deductions are poorly documented.

The new Taxpayer's Rights law also provides for an ombudsman in its Problem Resolutions Office to help resolve disputes between you and the IRS. It is to your advantage as well as the IRS's to cut down on red tape and reach an equitable agreement in a reasonable amount of time, so keep that in mind when dealing with any aspect of an IRS audit.

CHAPTER FIVE
TROUBLESHOOTERS

Q. *I keep a log in my car's glove compartment to write down business miles driven. Since I drive to my studio every morning from home in this car, can I deduct the miles I drive to work and back as a business expense?*

A. Sorry, but the IRS doesn't allow you to deduct the costs of your commute to work. You should log as business miles only the trips necessary for conducting business *after* you've arrived at work (driving to client meetings, to get supplies, etc.)

Q. *I understand that it's important for me to keep good records for my studio, but I'm drowning in an ocean of paper! How long must I keep back records?*

A. You should keep accounting records for your business permanently. Under normal circumstances, the receipts and cancelled checks you use to support tax deductions can be thrown away three years after the return they support was filed. Beware, however, that if the IRS can prove that you knowingly concealed income or information from them, they can question deductions and ask for documentation as far back as they like—no limit.

The IRS has a general guideline of seven years for most documentation. Your accountant or attorney can give you a detailed list of how long to retain which records.

If retention/storage space is a problem, there are firms that will keep your records for you at their own warehouse-like facilities. If you have the need for a file they have, you tell them the box number and they retrieve and deliver it right to your door.

Q. *I did some in-house work for a company, and they sent me a 1099 form listing my fee as "miscellaneous income." That's fine, but the amount was listed as double what I was actually paid. What should I do?*

A. The information on Form 1099 goes directly to the IRS, and if the amount you report on your return is different than what the business reported it paid you, a red flag goes up. Have the company refile a corrected 1099 with the IRS, and then on your tax return, list the old, incorrect amount under income, but calculate the difference, and list it under deductions as a "1099 error." Enclose a letter with your return explaining the error and how it was corrected.

CHAPTER FIVE
CHECKLISTS

Do you need a tax planner? The legal structure of your business determines how you calculate your taxes:
☐ A sole proprietor files a Form 1040 and Schedule C.
☐ An unincorporated partnership files an information (K1) return, and partners file separate personal returns reporting their share of profits.
☐ A corporation reports its income through a series of corporate income tax forms that should be filled out by an accountant.
☐ A sub-chapter S corporation reports corporate income on the principal owners' individual 1040 personal income tax returns.

Your studio must pay these taxes:
☐ Federal income tax.
☐ Social Security Self-employment tax.
☐ Unemployment tax.
☐ State and local taxes.

Keep accurate records of your studio's income and expenditures to:
☐ Document tax deductions.
☐ Monitor your studio's financial health.
☐ Price jobs more profitably.

What records to keep:
☐ Invoices.
☐ Receipts.
☐ Cancelled checks.
☐ Bank statements.
☐ Corporate credit card statements.
☐ Contracts.
☐ Letters confirming verbal agreements.
☐ Bank deposit and withdrawal slips.
☐ Monthly utility bills.

Recordkeeping is easier if you:
☐ Keep separate job files.
☐ Segregate business from personal finances.
☐ Ask that checks be made out in the company name, not yours.
☐ Pay bills by check from your business account or corporate charge card.
☐ Keep a daily expense journal for small items.
☐ Fill out a business auto use log.
☐ Supply details on business check stubs.
☐ Use a book of petty cash vouchers.
☐ Maintain a payroll journal for employees.

When filing a Schedule C, back up deductions with receipts and use the following categories:
☐ Advertising.
☐ Bad debts.
☐ Bank service charges.
☐ Car and truck expenses.
☐ Commissions.
☐ Depreciation.
☐ Dues and publications.
☐ Insurance.
☐ Legal and professional services.
☐ Office expenses.
☐ Rental or lease of machinery, etc.
☐ Taxes.
☐ Travel, meals and entertainment.
☐ Utilities.

In order to deduct the expenses of a home studio you must:
☐ Prove exclusive use.
☐ Prove regular use.
☐ Prove principal place of business.
☐ Determine what percentage of your home is studio space using square footage.

You may trigger an audit with:
☐ Questionable deductions.
  An accountant with many other
  audited clients.
☐ Numbers rounded to even hundred
  dollar amounts.
☐ A large, single deduction.
☐ Filing a sloppy return.

The Taxpayer Bill of Rights ensures
your right to:
☐ Be informed of your rights at all
  times during an audit.
☐ Send a representative in your place.
☐ Record audit proceedings.
☐ Schedule meetings with IRS agents
  according to your convenience.

Different kinds of audits include:
☐ Correspondence, handled through
  the mail, questioning a few items.
☐ Office, held at an IRS office, possibly
  questioning just a few items, generally more detailed than correspondence audit.
☐ Field examination, held at your studio, and more involved than a correspondence or office audit.
☐ Taxpayer Compliance Measurement Program, a full audit for which
  you are selected at random.

Survive an audit by:
☐ Not being afraid to bargain with IRS
  agents.
☐ Negotiating for a fair payment
  schedule.
☐ Hiring a tax representative.
☐ Talking with the ombudsman in the
  Problem Resolutions Office.

CHAPTER 6
PROMOTING YOUR STUDIO EFFECTIVELY

PROFIT POINTS

Make the right impression and generate more business by:

- Pinpointing the right prospects.
- Spending your promotional dollars wisely on cost-effective promotions.
- Spotting new marketing opportunities right under your nose.
- Realizing the long-term value of free work for a good cause.

Few individuals are born salespeople. But even if you don't see yourself as the kind of person who could sell an Eskimo a refrigerator, you should develop your marketing and self-promotion skills to a level that allows you to market your studio's work at profitable prices. This chapter is designed to give you a better understanding of the fundamental concepts and tools of marketing and self-promotion and make that part of your job easier.

If you know you aren't the marketing type, there is always the option of hiring a professional to handle your promotional needs. But you'll still need a basic understanding of marketing and promotional processes in order to evaluate candidates for the job and manage the implementation of a professional's marketing plan for your studio. The bottom line is that in order for your studio to thrive and profits to grow, you must know how to sell your designs or be able to hire and direct someone with the expertise to do so.

In addition to the ultimate goal of bringing in more business and building profits, two other important marketing goals are to relay your company's professional and personal level of integrity and to establish a level of consistency and confidence between your studio and the public.

If there is a single key to successful marketing of designs, it is *regularity of effort*. If you handle marketing efforts yourself, you should spend at least 30 percent of your time doing promotional work, whether that time is spent making telephone calls, designing promotional brochures, composing form letters, or meeting with potential clients to show your portfolio. Especially with letters and other mailings, regular contact is essential: Get your studio's name in front of the right people as often as possible, and when they need a designer, your name will come to mind.

The worst mistake you can make is to neglect marketing because you're "too busy" with "more important" design work. The risk is that when you finally look up from your drafting table, you'll find that you have an inadequate number of projects pending. It is important that you keep the marketing goals you established in your business plan always in the forefront. You must work these marketing efforts into your schedule, and set weekly goals ("This week I will call seven new potential annual report clients") to ensure that you don't put off marketing chores. Smaller, steady marketing efforts will always pay off better than a large, expensive, one-shot campaign.

TARGETING THE RIGHT MARKETS
Pinpointing the right customers for your designs isn't easy. You want to do work that maximizes both your profits and your own work satisfaction. Remember that in targeting a market, you're not only looking for the best-paying jobs, but also the most satisfying ones. Clients who can fulfill both needs *are* out there; it's just a matter of finding them.

Use both your own personal preferences and your own design experience to decide what kinds of clients and types of jobs to pursue. For instance, you may find that you like working for smaller, emerging businesses rather than corporate giants, pharmaceutical companies rather than sporting goods manufacturers, corporate identity clients rather than environmental design jobs. Then look at your studio's job file records. Which clients have provided your studio with the most profitable work in the past? Balancing your own preferences against client profitability profiles, develop an idea of a type, or better yet, several types of clients to pursue.

The Prospective Client List
With a profile in mind of what type of clients you'd like, finding the right companies is much easier. To identify firms that you'd like to work for and that may need your services, develop the habit of processing all information with an eye to marketing your design skills. It may be

as simple as keeping your eyes and ears open. For example:

■ You've decided that you want to do more work for entertainment-oriented companies, and you read in your local newspaper that a multi-screen movie house is being built nearby. Contact the management company for possible signage and print ad work.

■ You're trying to develop more small retail clients, and you hear at a cocktail party that someone's cousin's maternity wear boutique is in a sales slump. Propose a new ad campaign to the owner to help boost sales.

■ You want to do more designs for professionals, and your stepson tells you that his girlfriend has decided to leave the law firm where she has been working to start her own firm. Who better to design the firm's logo and stationery than you?

■ You read a trade magazine article describing a new line of merchandise that an old client of yours is introducing. Call any contacts you have in the company to find out how far along packaging and ad designs are, and let them know you have some interesting ideas for their line that you'd like to discuss.

Here are some of the best avenues for developing a prospective client list:

■ Friends, colleagues, and acquaintances.
■ Trade journals and associations.
■ Community service/business groups (such as your city's chamber of commerce and local community service clubs).
■ The yellow pages.
■ Industry listings.
■ Former clients.

Once you've decided whom you'd like to work for, and what you'd like to be doing, there are a number of sources for information about potential clients. The best way to impress a prospective client is to be knowledgeable about and interested in their business. Some

resources to investigate *before* you meet with the client are:

■ Annual reports available at libraries or through your stock broker or brokerage house.
■ Local news items.
■ Trade magazines.

These sources provide you with background knowledge of the company, product profiles, prior design styles used, and names of key contact people.

If you plan to market to a certain industry, it is essential to understand that industry well. How is it doing in the current economic climate? In what ways do firms in the industry use design? What personality traits are admired in this business? Do most people in the industry share similar values and attitudes? If so, what are they? Who are the customers in this industry, and what are they like? These are just a few of the aspects of an industry that you should understand before trying to market to it. A major advantage to this specialty marketing is that your studio begins to develop a level of expertise within the industry, much like a bakery is known for its wedding cakes or a cardiologist is consulted about heart problems rather than other ailments.

Try putting yourself in the potential customer's shoes. Aren't you more likely to buy a piece of clothing in a shop where the salesperson asks what you're looking for, helps you choose items in the appropriate size, and takes into account your body size and age when suggesting different items? When trying to market your designs, you should be able to show such an in-depth understanding of the prospective client and its industry.

DEVELOPING A MARKETING PLAN

Once you have decided which companies you plan to market to, you must formulate a plan of action for developing them into clients. Depending on the kind and volume of work your studio produces, and which self-promotional

PERSONAL PROFILE

LONNIE ZWERIN
Marketing Consultant
San Francisco, California

"In thinking about marketing, you should start with a long look at your own studio. What kind of work do you like best? Which projects have proven to be the most profitable for your studio? And what sorts of design come most easily and naturally to you—what are you good at? From there, you will begin to get an idea of whom to focus your marketing efforts on," says Lonnie Zwerin, an independent consultant for marketing and creative services management who has worked for various design firms and other companies in the San Francisco Bay Area.

Zwerin feels that a client and vendor database is probably the single most important marketing tool a designer can maintain. She suggests coding the clients by industry, so if you do decide to do an industry-specific mailing, the correct companies can be easily culled out of the mailing list.

"Former clients can be a very effective marketing tool for a designer. After all, who better to recommend your work—or to use your design services again—than someone you've worked for before?" says Zwerin. "I recommend to many of the people I advise that they maintain a client list, and give everyone on it a call every few months or so, just to check in. Ask if there are any upcoming design projects that you could be of help in planning (and executing, of course), and if not, ask if the client has colleagues, either in the same company or elsewhere, who may be looking for a designer."

Zwerin feels that choosing either a particular industry to market your designs to or a type of design to specialize in may not be the best strategy for a small studio. "Most smaller studios still operate as generalists, and that is probably just as well. Demand from individual industries and for particular products can fluctuate wildly in the current economic climate, and a good designer can be left high and dry if suddenly the only industry or product he or she specializes in runs into trouble," she notes.

Another marketing tool that Zwerin recommends for designers is case studies. A case study is a brief outline of what you did for a former client with the measurable impact of

your design work noted after each project is completed. For instance, if you designed a series of print ads for a restaurant and sales increased 10 percent during the month the ads ran in the local newspaper, note that fact in the case study. Then the next time you are making a presentation to a restaurant chain to redesign its logo, show them the other restaurant work you've done and use facts from the case study to back up your claim that your designs get results. For most clients, financial results are more important than the cleverness of your designs.

Zwerin notes that the introduction of computer design software has made it harder for designers to market their services to some companies. "Because many companies now have design programs in-house, suddenly they are questioning the need to hire an outside designer at all. It is important to show them that although they may have a computer design *program*, they don't have a *designer*, and that you can work with the company's program, complementing its enhanced design capabilities with your expertise. The company's new design power needs to be harnessed and managed by a professional. Make the company see that now that it has improved graphics capabilities, it needs a designer even more than it did before. Otherwise, you may be left out of the whole desktop publishing revolution."

Look at a marketing plan as you would a production schedule, Zwerin suggests. For a design project, you must meet a series of smaller deadlines to complete it —doing preliminary sketches, choosing a typeface, taking and developing photographs, ordering color separations. To reach a marketing goal, plan and execute the smaller steps in the same manner. You might call ten prospective clients this week, write a letter to send to clients in a certain industry group, research ideas for a new promotional brochure, and revamp your portfolio as steps toward attracting five new clients this year.

"If you think of marketing as just a series of smaller projects to complete, it doesn't become this looming, shapeless task that hangs over your head indefinitely. The tasks involved in selling your design services become a regular part of your workday. A series of small, continuous efforts will do more for marketing your business than the most expensive, all-encompassing, one-shot ad campaign ever could," says Zwerin.

tools you plan to use, the marketing plan can range from simply mailing promotional brochures periodically to making sales calls and giving complex presentations.

The first thing you need to do is go back to the broad, strategic goals you set forth in your business plan. Whether you use sales figures (Goal: Total sales of $90,000 this year) or just a description of how you'd like your business to develop (Goal: At least 50 percent print ad work this year), put your strategic goals in writing, and constantly refer to them when developing your marketing plan.

After you've set these broader goals, establish shorter-term, more concrete goals to strive for as steps toward your strategic objectives. For example, if you'd like to design more annual reports for health care providers, consider setting a broad goal of getting two new corporate identity clients in the health care sector in the next year. Toward that end, set a shorter-term goal of sending out an industry-specific letter to the public relations departments of twenty-five health care providers, and of remailing similar promotional pieces once every two months for the next eight months. Setting these smaller, tactical goals to help reach a larger, strategic marketing goal is basically what "formulating a marketing plan" is all about.

For many companies, a marketing plan *is* an involved project, but for a small studio, what you're actually doing is setting up more of a marketing *schedule* than an actual marketing plan. In other words, once you decide whom to target, your marketing plan is simply an efficient way to keep track of whom you have contacted and their responses, and to plan follow-up procedures.

A marketing plan and promotional campaign of any size cannot be successful without two basic tools: a marketing calendar and a prospective-client recordkeeping system.

For a marketing calendar, use a large, block-style calendar with a page per month and plenty of writing space in each individual day's block. On this calendar, you should keep a record of any marketing-related action to be taken on a particular date. For instance, April 3rd might contain the following notes: "Follow-up calls to MEF Industries, Waters Inc., Adinolfi Associates and the Goody-Goody Co. Mail out health club targeted promo letter. Begin design for client holiday greeting card."

A system for tracking prospects is also essential. If possible, computerize the "prospects" list, so information can be easily updated and mailing labels printed out directly from your list. Whether a prospect list is on screen or simply written on 3 × 5 cards and kept in a recipe file box, each entry should include the company name, your contacts there (art director, PR people, etc.), the address and telephone number, and a dated record of all interactions with the company. For instance, MEF Industries' card, after naming contacts and recording the address and telephone number, might read like this:

- 4-13-91 — Mailed medical waste management targeted brochure.
- 4-22-91 — Spoke with Phil Wilson, director of PR. Requested that I recontact in one month.
- 5-20-91 — Called Wilson, who said he would consult CEO about new ad campaign for trade magazine. Call in one week.
- 5-26-91 — Scheduled interview and portfolio review for 6-4-91.

As your business develops, formulating and working with a marketing plan will become easier. You'll gain a clearer idea of how and when to contact potential clients, what to say, and how to chart your marketing efforts simply and regularly. The important thing is to *have* a marketing plan and to make marketing efforts a regular part of your business day. After a while, making contact calls will become as natural to you as choosing a typeface, and your studio's profits will show you how important both design *and* marketing skills are to the health of your studio.

USING MAILING LISTS

Many designers use promotional letters, brochures, and regular mailings to promote their services. Since most design work can be displayed on the printed page or in photographs, promotional mailings are a great opportunity for designers to illustrate their services and design styles and promote their studios.

Most designers agree that *regular* mailing of promotional materials to a select group of potential buyers of their services (art directors, PR people, or small-company presidents) is the most effective method of promotion. Whether the mailing is a clever postcard, a simple letter with a four-color brochure, or a three-dimensional "freebie" such as a calendar or other small gift, designers find that gentle, regular reminders of their design capabilities help to get them the most clients.

As far as the design of the mailing piece goes, almost anything can work if it is well-devised. For ideas, you can consult books such as *The Graphic Artist's Guide to Marketing and Self-Promotion*, by Sally Prince Davis, *Promo 1*, by Rose deNeve (both published by North Light Books), and recent self-promotion awards issues of design magazines for examples of promotional pieces designed to get results.

Assuming you have designed and printed a terrific promotional piece for your studio, where do you send it? Marketing experts agree that, especially for a smaller studio, its own in-house client mailing list is the most important marketing tool it has. Include on this list former clients, prospects, suppliers and other businesses whose services you have bought, and any companies you are familiar with in a specific niche you have targeted. Keeping such a list on a personal computer makes it much easier to add new names and delete old ones, and when you are ready to mail, you can print the names directly onto mailing labels. Update the list at least monthly, adding to it names of people you have met at industry conferences, by networking, or through other outlets.

Another idea to consider is trading or sharing your in-house mailing list with someone in a business related to design, like a printer or photographer. A client who needs a printer often also needs a designer.

If you feel your in-house list isn't large or diverse enough to help you attract the type or number of new clients you're after, you may want to rent a mailing list from a list broker. The key to using a mailing list effectively is knowing both the business *and* the contact person you wish to sell to. In other words, the better targeted the mailing list, the more likely your promotional pieces will reach the people who both like your designs and have the authority to contract for your services.

To this end, it is important to pinpoint *who* in the companies you are targeting is actually in a position to purchase design services. For example, if you mail to art directors of large pharmaceutical houses, and then find out that the public relations managers are the people who choose designers and the art director simply acts as a coordinator in these types of firms, you may end up impressing a great many art directors but getting no jobs. You'll not only waste your efforts, but also most of your promotional budget.

It helps to mail to firms in specific industries for which you have worked before or for which you would like to work. Depending on how much you know about an industry, you may even want to design a mailing piece specifically for a certain industry subsector, such as restaurant chains, academic publishers, or menswear retailers. Especially with smaller firms that may not be used to hiring and working with a designer, showing that you have worked for other companies in their field and understand it well can improve your chances of winning them as a client.

The more targeted a rented mailing list is, the more effective it will be, but also the more expensive it is to rent. A list broker will send you a catalog of the lists they rent, with different prices for single use and unlimited use during a limited time period. There are even list brokers that specialize in lists for graphic artists and design firms such as Creative Access in Chicago. Inquire how often they update

PERSONAL PROFILE

DAVID BRIER
DBD International Limited
Rutherford, New Jersey

"Because so many designers are uncomfortable with the marketing aspects of running a studio, they tend to give the designing of their own promotion pieces short shrift," observes David Brier, owner and principal designer of DBD International Limited in Rutherford, New Jersey. "That's a fatal mistake, marketingwise, because often a promotional piece represents your studio more widely than any other work you do. And who wants to be represented by a design that was created using less than optimal creative energy and time? Not doing your best work for your own studio is like shooting yourself in the foot."

These days, it's clear that Brier's gun has been nowhere near his own sneakers. His clever promotional mailings have brought in such clients as Boardroom, Inc., the New York City Opera, *Rolling Stone*, Children's Television Workshop, Phoneworks, and design-industry clients such as the Society of Publication Designers and the Type Directors Club. His design awards are numerous. And he does it all himself, with the help of one design/production assistant and an administrative assistant.

A recent promotional mailing by DBD International Limited illustrates Brier's two golden rules for effective promotion pieces: they must be fun, and responding to them must be as easy as possible. The triple-accordion-folded, small-envelope-sized piece urges clients to join in the fight against recycled designs. Cans and bottles are fine to reuse, the piece states, but recycled design is just the "same old garbage." The mailing includes a "membership card" for People Against Recycled Design, which carries a pledge that as a member in good standing, the person will never use recycled designs. It gives a telephone number to call for "the original design supplier nearest you," which just happens to be, of course, DBD's Rutherford, New Jersey studio.

The mailing also contains a business reply card, an aspect of promotional mailing about which Brier is dead serious. "Besides reaching people and making them chuckle, you must also make their response as effortless as possible," he notes. "One of the most frequent mistakes I see in other promotional mailings is the assumption that just because a piece is amusing and well designed, its recipient will pick up the phone. Businesspeople are busy, and you must make their reply as easy as handing a postage-free reply card to their secretary."

Brier is also a great believer in maintaining and using in-house mailing lists. He keeps three separate lists on computer: a client list, a list of companies that have expressed interest in DBD's design work in the past, and a list of companies he's interested in working for. Some mailings are designed for only one of the lists, while a piece such as the "recycled design" promo is mailed to all three.

"In the years I've been in business, I've learned something very important about how marketing and design interact," says Brier. "Clients hire designers mostly for marketing reasons, whether it is to design a book cover, a corporate identity, packaging, or a publication. They use a designer because they want their product to sell better. With this in mind, it stands to reason that most clients would prefer a designer that shows an ability to market his or her own designs effectively. If a designer appears to lack marketing talent, it just might be that his or her designs won't be that effective in marketing the cli-

their lists and what level of accuracy they guarantee. If, for example, the names sold to the mailing list company are already six months or a year old and the mailing company only updates every year (if at all), there is no guarantee the person you are trying to contact is actually the person still in that position at that company.

Do not add the rented list names to your studio's in-house list, because to do so is considered theft. However, if, after an initial mailing, a firm from a rented list contacts you for more information, that company becomes yours and should be entered on your own in-house mailing list as a prospective client.

ent's product successfully. Clients know that good marketing and good design go hand in hand, and a talented designer should know that as well."

But first-class promo pieces cost money, don't they? Brier thinks that the cost of a top-notch promotional piece is money well spent—a solid investment in the future of any studio. He also points out that there are ways to cut costs. He suggests, "Look for creative and money-saving solutions when designing a promo piece within a budget. For instance, suppose you are supervising the printing of a job for a client, and you notice that an 11 × 14 inch section of paper will be discarded from the final product. Why not design a promotional piece to fit the space of that leftover paper, pay for the prep work, and save yourself the extra printing costs?"

Brier admits that he used to be afraid to really let go, both in his design work and in his marketing efforts. But once he saw that he did his best work in both areas only when he pulled out all the stops, he began to make his own wackiness a company trademark. "I try to challenge preconceived notions when working with a client. When a person tells me, 'Because it should be that way' or 'Because we've always done it that way,' I take that as a direct challenge to find a better way to handle a design problem. In all aspects of my business, I try to avoid tunnel vision."

Besides mailing promotional pieces, Brier also generates publicity for his studio by speaking at conferences and seminars. And he is one of those strange types that actually *enjoys* making cold sales calls. "I see good marketing as the *reason* I get to make designs," Brier says, "and for this reason alone, the time I devote to it is definitely time well spent."

WHICH SELF-PROMOTION TOOLS ARE RIGHT FOR YOU?

There are a variety of ways in which you can represent and promote your studio's work. Following is a list of the most common self-promotion tools, and some advice about how to use each one most effectively:

■ *Business cards and stationery.* These may be the first and only contact many potential clients have with your design work. For this reason, both the design and the printing must be impeccable. If you have a diversity of clients, you may want to design several different letterheads and business cards slanted at different market segments—a classic look for corporate clients, something more experimental for entrepreneurs and artistic clients. You can play around with the business card form as well—a double-sized, folded card with your name, address, and phone number on the front and a simple list of the kinds of design services you provide printed inside can be very effective. Remember, first impressions are lasting impressions and it is important that your logo and the design of your business cards (and accompanying stationery) reflect your design style and creativity. After all, those are the skills you want people to know about and come to you for.

■ *A standard studio brochure.* Not to be confused with promotional mailing pieces, this brochure should be designed to profile your studio in detail. Beside being a showcase for your design talents, the standard brochure should reflect your design philosophy, provide a list of services, describe your rates and terms, and mention your areas of expertise, former and present clients, and any design awards your studio has won. Have plenty of copies to give to anyone who is interested, and you might even send several copies to clients so they can pass them on to their business associates.

■ *Promotional mailing pieces.* These can range from simple postcards to three-dimensional extravaganzas. The possibilities for such promotional pieces are endless, but whatever form they take, make sure their design reflects your best work. A number of designers have been very successful with regular mailings of funny and clever promo pieces to a lucky list of prospects. The contacts eagerly look forward to the next piece, and certainly will remember the studio the next time they need a designer, or hear of someone else who does.

Just as it's important for you as a designer to produce cost-effective designs for clients, it's important to consider cost of production for your own promotional pieces. It's easy to get carried away on a piece you want to use to show off your own creativity, but it's important to work within a reasonable budget you establish for the project. You should also consider the costs of reaching potential clients. Directories and contests are effective ways of reaching clients, and cooperating with other designers to create direct mail pieces can help you cut expenses. Information about these promotional possibilities is given below.

■ *Creative services books.* These directories of designers usually list the company name and principal designers, the studio's design capabilities and areas of expertise, and show examples of the studio's work. This kind of advertising certainly reaches a very targeted market of people who have both the power to hire designers and the need to do so; however, because it is so effective, a trade book listing can be very expensive. Before deciding to advertise in a creative services book, make sure your studio is well-established and able to afford such a sum for marketing. Also make sure you have top-notch examples of your designs to use in the ad, and that the book is going to the kinds of companies you wish to work for.

■ *Design contests.* Contests can be a great way to get your work in front of a wider audience, and any design awards you win should be mentioned in your company brochure. Look for contests sponsored by design magazines and industry guilds and organizations.

■ *Promotional collaboration.* Another method of handling promotion for your studio is to form a promotional collaboration yourself. For instance, you might want to design a promotional mailing piece with other designers to promote the services of each member of the group. A collaborative design on one side and examples of each person's work shown separately on the other, with name, address and phone number under each design, can be an eye-catching alternative to the same old promo postcards or letters. In such a collaboration, not only are design and printing costs shared, but you can also form a mutual mailing list, composed of each member's in-house list. For many studios, a cooperative approach to designing and mailing a promo piece can bring great results.

THE VALUE OF LONG-TERM RETURN ON "FREEBIE" WORK

One sure-fire way to increase your studio's exposure in your community is to donate your services for local design jobs. But choose such freebies carefully, and budget only the time you can devote to them without eating too deeply into your own profits. Playbills for community theatre groups, brochures for local museum exhibits and posters for charity events can provide your studio with maximum exposure to people in the local artistic community. These kinds of people are often the ones with the power to hire a designer in their nine-to-five positions.

Another way to bolster your design reputation in the community is to offer a free, one-day workshop in basic lay-out skills to a local business group. Besides adding a feather to your cap, you will meet a whole classroom full of entrepreneurs, public relations people, and others interested in design. The next time they need to hire a designer for a project, they may very well think of you.

HIRING A MARKETING CONSULTANT OR PR PERSON

Not to be confused with a sales representative (see Chapter Seven for advice on how to choose and use a sales rep), a marketing or public relations consultant is hired by a designer to help snag a client's initial interest. If you decide you need outside help in marketing and publicizing your studio's designs, be aware that choosing a consultant can be especially tricky. Marketing experts tend to be *marketing* experts, who may be more effective at hyping their own consulting practice than actually marketing a designer's work. On the other hand, if a marketing pro can sell his services to you well, that may be a sign that he or she will also be able to sell your services effectively.

Following are guidelines for choosing the right consultant to market your designs:

■ *Ask associates and competitors for advice.* Ask for recommendations, and make appointments with a few different consultants/firms. Your first consultation should be free of charge.

■ *In your first meeting, look for a marketer who listens more than she talks.* Initially, a good promoter should be more interested in finding out what your studio is like and whether her marketing style fits your way of doing things than in trying to sell you on using her services.

■ *Choose a full-service marketing/advertising/public relations agency.* Such an agency can look at your studio and your marketing goals, and the current market for your designs, and formulate and execute a complete marketing effort for you.

■ *Pick an agency that has experience with designers and/or smaller businesses.* You don't want to end up with advice that is unsuitable for the art market or unusable in a smaller company.

■ *Ask the consultant or agency to draw up a marketing plan* (with a budget of $1,500 or less for a small studio) and then discuss which elements you'd like to implement first. No marketing plan should be swallowed hook, line and sinker. Make sure you understand the rationale for each step in the marketing process and that you fully approve of it before you agree to it. Feel free to accept parts of the plan while vetoing others.

■ *Include yourself and your employees in the implementation of the plan.* Ask to be taught how to approach marketing research, press releases and mailings. Your direct involvement in the marketing process will both teach you marketing skills and ensure that, in the midst of all this selling, the quality and character of your studio remains intact.

CHAPTER SIX
TROUBLESHOOTERS

Q. *Believe it or not, my last mailing was too successful. I've suddenly been swamped with calls from all kinds of corporate clients to design in-house newsletters using desktop publishing software. I'm getting a little bored doing only these types of jobs. What should I do?*

A. First, count your blessings. The response was not only a confirmation of your excellent design skills, but one that can open doors to other design projects these clients might have besides the newsletters. Keep this experience in mind when you put together your next promotional brochure. Try to refocus the copy in your promotional material to appeal to the kinds of companies that are both interesting and profitable to you, and emphasize other areas of design in which you'd like to do more work. You might consider mailing to a smaller, more select list of potential clients next time as well.

Q. *I understand how important marketing is to my small graphics studio. The problem is that I am terrible at it, and I can't really afford the fees a good marketing consultant charges. Help!*

A. First of all, take a look at what you do as a designer. You are essentially helping other companies in any one of a hundred ways to market their products or services. Take on that mindset when you think about marketing your own skills. If you still feel you need help, there are two potential low-cost solutions to your problem. First, you could improve your own marketing skills by reading a good marketing textbook or taking a class on marketing tactics at your local community college or Small Business Administration office. A mar-

keting seminar run by a design association could be very helpful. If you really feel ill-prepared, you might hire a business manager/marketer/sales representative on staff. Look for someone who is young, has a lot of energy, and is interested in growing with your studio, rather than an experienced marketing whiz whose salary you can't afford. Marketing help that is slightly less experienced but bright and enthusiastic is certainly better than none at all.

Q. *I hired a well-known marketing group in my town, and paid them $4,000 for a terrific marketing plan that included market research, brochures with photographs, and even ad placement services. The problem is that I suddenly feel like a stranger in my own studio. Their work didn't reflect my design studio—it could have been someone else's. The marketing efforts were effective and I have lots of new business, but they feel phoney. Should I just ride with the new wave of business and be thankful?*

A. Yes. But next time try to choose a marketing consultant that understands a little more about your business and your design style. Especially in a business such as design, clients need to understand the aesthetic and temperament of the studio providing the design service. Clients need to feel confident that your designs can best represent their company and project the image they want. If your marketing efforts don't represent your studio's character accurately, you may find yourself with clients who want images totally different from the ones you're most able at creating, and you may end up doing designs you're proud of, but that your clients don't appreciate.

CHAPTER SIX
CHECKLISTS

Marketing goals:
- ☐ Convey integrity.
- ☐ Establish consistency.
- ☐ Include regularity of effort.
- ☐ Parallel goals in business plan.

There are several ways to target a market:
- ☐ Classify potential clients by the type of business they are in or the type of design job you want to do for them.
- ☐ Use information from past job files to decide which types of projects have been most profitable for your studio.
- ☐ Develop the habit of always looking out for new potential clients.
- ☐ Understand the industry your target clients are in.

Sources to consider for potential prospects:
- ☐ Friends, colleagues and acquaintances.
- ☐ Community business groups.
- ☐ Industry directory listings.
- ☐ Former clients.
- ☐ Annual reports.
- ☐ Local news articles.
- ☐ Trade magazines.

Develop a marketing plan by:
- ☐ Setting broad, strategic goals consistent with your business plan.
- ☐ Moving toward these goals with shorter-term steps.
- ☐ Setting up a marketing plan or schedule just as you would set a production schedule for a design project.
- ☐ Using a marketing calendar and a prospective client tracking system.

Use mailing lists more effectively by:
- ☐ Using well-designed marketing materials; look at current design annuals to see good examples.
- ☐ Maintaining an in-house list of former, current and potential clients to mail promo pieces to.
- ☐ Sharing in-house lists with other design-related businesses.
- ☐ Renting mailing lists, which are most effective if specifically narrowed to an industry you'd like to sell to and addressed directly to the person in the company who buys creative services.
- ☐ Adding a name from a rented list to your in-house list only if the prospect contacts you after an initial mailing.

Self-promotion tools include:
- ☐ Business cards and stationery.
- ☐ Standard brochures.
- ☐ Promotional mailing pieces.
- ☐ Creative services books.
- ☐ Design contests.
- ☐ A collaborative promotional piece with other designers.
- ☐ Pro bono work—"freebie" jobs that give your designs high profile and associate them with the local artistic community.
- ☐ Leading workshops, giving guest lectures and speeches.

When hiring a marketing consultant or PR person:
- ☐ Ask colleagues and friends for recommendations.
- ☐ Choose a marketer who listens more than he or she talks.
- ☐ Use a full-service marketing/advertising/public relations agency.
- ☐ Look for someone with small-business or design-firm experience.
- ☐ Ask for a prioritized marketing plan using a limited budget.
- ☐ Handle any aspect of the market plan that you can in-house.

CHAPTER 7

HOW TO MAKE CLIENT-WINNING PRESENTATIONS

PROFIT POINTS

Win the clients you want by:

- Communicating clearly on paper and in person.
- Choosing visuals that will attract and keep your client's attention.
- Customizing your presentations for prospective clients.
- Tackling and overcoming common obstacles to effective selling.

When you make a client presentation, you are in effect asking the client to buy something he cannot see, hear, touch, smell or taste: your design ideas. With this in mind, the reason why your client presentations are your most important marketing tool should be clear. The presentation is your best opportunity to show the client what he will actually be buying *before* the final designs are delivered, and as such, it should be given your best marketing and creative energies. Throughout your presentation you should let your client see examples of your work, feel your style, and sense your design abilities.

Too many designers throw together a proposal the night before a client meeting and count on their portfolios to speak for them. The problem with this approach is that your client presentation ends up stressing what you've done for *other* companies rather than showing what you plan to do for the prospective client. A carefully written proposal that indicates you have researched the client's design needs and particular problems will do much more to convince a potential design services buyer that you understand the company's needs and can get results *for that particular client* with your designs. It is important to show solutions and provide answers in your presentation. Today's buyers no longer buy products or services; they buy solutions and answers.

CUSTOMIZING YOUR PORTFOLIO

Rather than have a standard portfolio that you use for all prospective clients or a series of industry specific portfolios, each time you present your work you should carefully assemble a customized portfolio that will be most effective for that particular client. For this reason, your portfolio pieces must be mounted or laminated separately. Alternatively, you can have your work photographed and made into slides, which can be used in different combina-

tions to make up portfolios that are suitable for each presentation.

Although your design pieces will be of different sizes, mount them on uniformly sized boards if possible, so they can be clipped or tied together in binder form if necessary. You can even mount several smaller, related designs on the same board. This approach can help make a rather disparate group of designs look orderly.

Obviously, any portfolio you compose should only contain your best work. Don't be afraid to limit the portfolio to a small number of samples, even just five or six. If you're worried that a prospective client may find your sampling scanty, remember that five terrific pieces *always* make a more impressive portfolio than five great pieces plus seven mediocre ones.

If you drop off or mail a portfolio, your studio's logo should appear on the back of all boards and you should always enclose a company brochure and a business card. And no portfolio should ever leave your studio without your noting on your marketing calendar when to make a follow-up call or visit. (See Chapter Six for how to use a marketing calendar.)

HOW TO SAY EXACTLY WHAT YOU WANT TO SAY

Before we even begin to discuss how to make a client presentation, here are a few hints for communicating more effectively whenever you deal with clients, prospects, or even co-workers and colleagues. While the following points will be helpful, you may also want to buy and study a book on effective business communication, especially if you know this is a weakness of yours. Remember that your designs can only do a certain amount of communicating for you; although your best method of communication may be visual, it can't be your only method. For more effective written and verbal communication:

■ *Make sure both your written and spoken grammar is impeccable.* You don't want clients focusing on your mistakes rather than on the ideas you're trying to convey through your language.

■ *Do your homework, and remind yourself that you are well-prepared before speaking publicly.* If you know your stuff, you're more likely to express yourself clearly and confidently. Clarity and confidence are two characteristics clients often look for when choosing someone to do visual communications by designing for their company.

■ *Don't rush.* Especially in spoken communication, people tend to speed up when they get nervous. If, for instance, a client raises an objection that catches you off guard, don't be afraid to pause a moment to collect your thoughts before answering. Your answer will be stronger for the few seconds of silence, and you run less risk of blurting out a defensive retort. If you don't know the answer to a client's question, admit that, and let him know that you'll have the answer as soon as possible.

■ *In written communication, don't try to make the first draft perfect.* Instead, just jot down the major points you want to cover, and in what ways you want to cover them. *Then* go back and polish the language. Don't let the editor in you kill the writer in you.

■ *Write to express, not impress.* The days of stilted, overblown business language are over. Use simple, straightforward, familiar words to say what you mean. Examples: "I have been made aware of" becomes "I know," "In the event that the preliminary sketches do not meet with your approval" should be "If the early sketches are unsatisfactory."

■ *Avoid tentative-sounding or passive language.* Passive language used to be understood as a sign of politeness or respect; now it just sounds wishy-washy. Replace "Your company was suggested to me by Rhonda Bly" with "Rhonda Bly suggested you," "Perhaps our companies could work together productively" with "I have great design ideas for your firm."

■ *Make sure there are no typos.* It is a good idea to have several people proofread final documents before they go out the door. Nothing gives a client a negative impression more than professional documents (especially brochures or proposals) with typographical errors. If your own work goes out that way, a prospect can only draw the conclusion that you'll be just as careless with her work.

■ *Don't be perfect—be yourself.* Although you must make sure that you are well-prepared with facts and that you give a coherent, intelligent presentation of your ideas, don't be obsessed with expressing everything perfectly. If you are, you will tend to fixate on the inevitable small mistakes in your writing or speech and freeze up, invariably making more mistakes in the process. Instead, focus on presenting your ideas in a style that feels natural to you—even if every phrase isn't perfect.

CONTACTING CLIENTS

From the first time you hear of a company to the successful mounting of a marketing campaign using your designs, how you relate to clients is almost as important as how good your designs are. If you aren't able to work well with the people you are working for, or hope to work for, you may end up not working at all. This next section takes you through the most common types of dealings you will have with clients and suggests ways of handling those situations more effectively and profitably.

Cold Telephone Calls

For many people, the initial telephone call is the hardest part of dealing with clients. Because they feel embarrassed and overly aggressive at the same time when calling up a stranger or acquaintance, they can find any number of chores to use as excuses to avoid picking up the receiver. But cold calls are an important way to keep abreast of what's happening in your local community as well as in the design market, and to sniff out new clients.

Whether you are talking to the receptionist or to the art director or creative services buyer, be clear about who you are and why you're call-

PERSONAL PROFILE

JOHN MELCHINGER
Consultant and Newsletter Publisher
Tampa, Florida

"Many designers have what they think is a problem for making client presentations—a reserved, low-key personality. In fact, such a personality can be a plus in dealing with clients. When what you are 'selling' to a client is your ability to solve the client's communication/marketing problem with your design work, being a good listener is more important than being a flashy speaker," observes John Melchinger, a Tampa, Florida-based marketing and business consultant for personal services companies nationwide.

Melchinger feels that the first interview, which should be a fact-finding session with the company, is in some ways more important than the second meeting, in which designers actually try to sell their design solutions. "At the first interview, since you haven't yet presented the company with any concrete design ideas, the only thing they have to judge you on is your manner. And the judgments tend to be emotional. If, at the first meeting, you are perceived as interested, a good listener, and capable of asking intelligent questions about the firm and its marketing strategy and processing the information you receive, then when you make your presentation in the second meeting, people will already see you as an ally in solving their problem. If not, they are much more likely to perceive you as a salesperson, and to put up all of the natural defenses that go along with that perception."

He suggests that designers with presentation stage fright develop a list of twelve key questions to ask in an initial interview: "Who do you sell to now and to whom do you plan to market?" "What are three common *mis*conceptions about your product, company or industry?" "How does color relate to your product—are there certain standard colors or design styles usually associated with it?" "Would you like to change that or create a new design that conforms to certain preconceived notions, yet adds a memorable spark of difference?" Melchinger notes that once the designer and company representatives get involved in a discussion about the product, the focus is no longer on the verbal skills of the artist, and he can relax and address the design possibilities rather than worry about being a whiz-bang salesperson.

Melchinger likens the presentation process to a court trial. "In a trial, you first do jury selection. In the presentation process, of course, you can't choose whom you will present to, but you can get an understanding of the preferences and prejudices of the people who will judge your campaign. This is what a lawyer does when he interviews prospective jurors." Then there are opening arguments, in which the facts of the case are presented to the jury by both lawyers and by the judge. This is equivalent to the fact-finding interview, when you try to understand the problem the company wants to address with your designs. Then, the lawyers present evidence and explain their arguments, and cross-examine each other's witnesses. A designer's presentation should be full of the 'evidence' of why his or her designs will be helpful to the client's marketing efforts, and explanations of why certain design decisions were made, based on what the designer learned about the product and company in the initial fact-finding meeting. Finally, the jury (or in our case, the company) decides whether to accept or reject the charges (design proposal).

"There is also a classic mistake that not only designers but businesspeople of all types make in presenting their ideas," says Melchinger. "They begin the presentation by reviewing the company's needs and marketing history, and then present their design solution as a plan for meeting those needs. The problem is that you start out by telling people something they already know (not to mention rubbing salt into old marketing-failure wounds), and these busy people become bored and then irritated while they wait to finally be given the meat of your presentation." In this case, Melchinger notes, your planned "big buildup" just makes your audience cranky when it's finally time to look at your designs. Try opening the presentation by showing your designs first, with a minimal amount of fanfare, and then while people scrutinize and discuss them, you can explain your design decisions in light of your in-depth knowledge of the product, the market, and the company's past successes and failures in marketing, plus your own design sense. This is a more efficient and effective way to use presentation time, and it will ensure that your designs get the good-spirited scrutiny they deserve.

ing. You might want to prepare both a short statement and a longer description of what your studio does. The short statement is to help secretaries transfer the call to the correct department; the longer pitch is to explain briefly who you are, what type of design you do, and why you're calling, so you can reach the correct person within a department.

When you do reach that person, get right to the point. Find out if she has a few minutes to talk, and if so, explain why you are calling ("I read in *Food Retailing Monthly* that you will be introducing a new line of snack cakes next year and I have several interesting design ideas for the packaging. May I send you a portfolio of my work?").

Add to this introduction any other connection you have with the firm ("My studio designed your firm's 1987 and 1988 annual reports" or "My colleague Nancy Butler suggested I call you since she enjoyed working on your departmental newsletter.")

Last but not least, be persistent. If your messages go unanswered, keep calling—and keep leaving polite messages—until you finally talk to the right person. And if that person suggests that you call back later, ask for a suggestion of when (A month? Six months? Tomorrow?), and make a note on your marketing calendar (see Chapter Six) to do so.

Portfolio Drop-Offs

First, make sure you understand whether the creative services buyer wants you to just drop off your work and leave, or prefers for you to stay around a few minutes for a brief meeting. In either case, show up on time, dressed neatly and professionally. You never know when you might just bump into someone who has input into the decision to contract for your design services.

Creative services buyers typically don't ask designers to drop off their portfolios unless they intend to at least meet them. Use those few moments to mention your studio's previous clients, specialties, and even say a word about your design philosophy. If your initial cold call wasn't about a specific design project, come prepared with other questions about the firm: What are its current design needs—in-house newsletter, annual report, product packaging, print ads, marketing materials? Do other departments within the company contract for designers as well? What are the company's marketing plans? Show that you are interested in working with the company to come up with terrific design solutions, and aren't just determined to sell them your work.

Before you leave, it is essential that you come to some kind of agreement about what the next step will be—a telephone conversation to schedule a time to pick up your portfolio after the person has had time to look it over, a chance to bid on a project, a review of new design samples in six months. *Always* plan a follow-up contact with the potential client, whether it is a call in three months, mailing a promotional piece, or simply sending a letter thanking the person for taking a look at your work. It usually takes at least four or five contacts with clients before you finally win the first assignment from them.

PUTTING TOGETHER AN EFFECTIVE PRESENTATION

The most common kind of client contact designers have is making client presentations or proposals. In fact, some designers spend as much time meeting and working with clients as they do on actual design work. But even if client meetings make up a smaller portion of your work time, it is still important that you know how to handle them well. Following is a recommendation for how to successfully go through the three-part presentation process.

The Initial Project Meeting

Although many designers focus on the proposal stage of a client presentation (see pages 100-101), the initial project meeting is in many ways even more important. In this meeting, you must ask the questions that will be most helpful to you in formulating a design strategy for the project.

This is not to say that you should go into the first meeting and say, "So, what does your company sell, anyway?" You'll need to do a certain amount of homework before meeting with the client, especially if you're not that familiar with the client's industry. Find out how the industry is doing in the current economy, where this firm fits in its industry, whether the product you are designing for is new or established, who buys it and why, and what kind of reputation the company has in the business community. (Are they pioneers or chance-takers, or is this a slow, steady growth company?) Keep in mind that even if you won't be designing an item that is sold directly to customers, the main goal of your design will result in a "sale" of some kind—otherwise the company would not be interested in designs at all. Figure out who "buys" the item and what kinds of things are attractive to that person. You'll have a much better chance of selling your designs to a client if you understand who you are talking to and what their concerns are.

A number of sources can give you a better idea of what makes a company tick. If possible, question your contact at the company by telephone. Talk to the firm's competitors. Go to the library to look for current and past articles about the firm, both in the mainstream press and in industry or trade publications. If you will be designing for a product already on the market (or if competitors have similar products on the market), think about what you (or potential customers) look for and like in such a product, and what values are usually attached to the sale of it. In other words, do some long, hard thinking about how your designs can work to help the product sell. And remember, even non-retail products must be "sold" to someone—an in-house newsletter must be designed for readability, an annual report must project the desired company image, a poster or letterhead must convey a certain style for the firm. Be careful not to focus on current designs your prospect is using. They obviously want a fresh approach; be sure to come up with one that is truly a departure from their old style.

In the initial meeting, don't be too anxious to show off all you know about the firm. Make it clear that you've done your homework: You know the firm and have formulated some ideas about how your designs can work to help it. But after establishing that, sit back and listen. Ask intelligent, probing questions about what they want to accomplish with your design work. Find out how they've done things in the past. Check on how long the creative director/art director or manager you are talking to has been at the company. A new manager or director may want to take a new approach. Also try to get a sense of who will be making the decisions about this project—understand the interplay of power between the project's team members, and figure out who you should be most concerned with pleasing.

It's wise to actively ask intelligent questions, but don't seem too aggressive or opinionated at this point. Although it may be hard to believe, sometimes the group you meet with hasn't *itself* clearly defined its goals and marketing tactics for a product, and you don't want to show them up as disorganized or vague. Put yourself into the role of team player *within* the project group, not that of judge of its strategy or merely a salesperson for your designs. Just the fact that you're interested in providing solutions to their design problems, and that you've researched the problems and the context, should do a lot to help them accept and appreciate your design work.

Leave the meeting with two things: An enhanced understanding of what they are looking for confirming the knowledge you gained to avoid any costly mistakes, and a clear idea of the next move. If the meeting ends with no resolution, find out when decisions concerning the use of your designs will be made and how you can help in the decision-making process by making yourself available—perhaps by being present at further meetings on the subject, sending more design samples, or calling the contact person for an answer next week. It might be appropriate to suggest a meeting between you, your contact, and his management/steering committee, so you can answer directly any questions they have. Don't be pushy, but do get a concrete idea of the next action to take.

PERSONAL PROFILE

JOE DUFFY
Duffy Design Group
Minneapolis, Minnesota

"There is a one-word secret to client-winning presentations: Homework! The more complete your understanding of the product's target audience, of the company's consumer profile, of its other products, and of the internal dynamic of the company's management, the more likely you are to win it as a client and provide it with terrific designs. That is it, pure and simple," says Joe Duffy, a partner and principal designer for the award-winning Duffy Design Group in Minneapolis, Minnesota.

Duffy's "homework" theory has won him straight *As* in the graphic design community. His studio has designed for such clients as Ralph Lauren, Porsche and Classico. Not bad for an eight-employee design firm that has just celebrated its seventh anniversary.

"So many designers believe that so long as their designs are good, that will be enough to win a client over. It just doesn't work that way," notes Duffy. "Even if clients *can* appreciate the artistic merit of a good design (and many of them can't), that still doesn't mean they'll buy your ideas. You must be able to prove to them not only that your design ideas are great, but that your designs will help boost *the sales of their product.* You must show that you understand the market they are pitching to and what kind of image the company wants to project to that market. If you can't prove your design work's marketability, then it probably belongs in a museum, not on a client's product."

Designers don't, however, necessarily have to be marketing experts. Duffy believes that the best sources of potential marketing strategies for the product are the company itself and its advertising agency. "Get involved; ask questions," he counsels. "Don't leave the client out of the design process. Instead, understand as much as you can from the company itself whom they are pitching to and what they believe appeals to that group of people. Then you can back up all of your design decisions with the marketing facts that lead you to make them."

Duffy has also found that there is another element designers often overlook when putting together a client presentation—who exactly has the power to hire them? Often the internal workings of a company are very complex, and you have a better chance of getting the job if you know to whom you should target your presentation. For example, are the young and friendly people you've been in communication with so far responsible as a group for making the hiring decision, or are they just fact-finders for an older, much more conservative CEO who controls all decisions within the company? As best you can, understand the interplay of power among all the people in the group you will be presenting to, and tailor your presentation accordingly.

"In general, the best work is done for the best clients," notes Duffy. "One part of your homework in putting together an initial client proposal should be to look at the design work from the company's earlier marketing efforts. If it is less than desirable, that may be a sign that either internal people were second-guessing the designer, or the people buying the company's design services just don't have good taste. Both are good reasons not to get involved with such clients."

Duffy finds case histories invaluable in helping to convince prospective clients that

Without insinuating yourself into the group in a sly way, you can still establish yourself as part of the team. You can make selecting your studio to handle the design work seem like a natural extension of your work with the company. This is a much better approach than trying to get the company to fall for your sales pitch.

Showing Your Proposed Design Solution

This is another stage of the presentation where many designers focus on their shortcomings as salespeople, and either freeze up or concoct an elaborate presentation style that may very well get in the way of effectively showing their designs. Instead, think of this phase of a presentation as two parts: the presentation of a his designs do get results. He says, "The Classico pasta sauce labels were the first food-packaging design job we had ever done. And they were enormously successful, boosting sales tremendously for the client. Because of that success, other food clients have been interested in us, and I always include a case history of the Classico project plus the company's resulting sales figures when I make a presentation to a food client. Even if you aren't able to get sales figures from a former client, a simple written profile of how the designs were used in a successful marketing campaign shows a prospective client that your work is effective as well as beautiful."

Duffy Design Group is also known for its ability to sell clients on a number of different design applications they may not have originally thought of. For example, Ralph Lauren originally hired the studio to design a "pocket billboard" (the stitched-on outer label on the back pocket of blue jeans and khakis). After the design work was done, Duffy and other staff members had a brainstorming session to come up with other possible applications for the design, and they sketched out a poster, a hang tag and a shirt band, all of which incorporated the original design. The company loved all the additional applications, and they ended up buying them. "The original design is usually the bulk of the work," says Duffy, "so it is often worth your while to give a few additional applications a shot, since it doesn't end up costing the studio that much in additional time and effort. And often the clients not only like the suggestions, they are thrilled that a designer is that involved in the total marketing effort."

written proposal, which the client can read over later, and the verbal presentation of the actual design.

The written proposal should be prepared carefully, and enough copies made for all members of the marketing team. It should contain:

■ *Introduction*. Outline briefly what was dis-

cussed in the initial project meeting.

■ *Background on your studio*. This should be a brief sketch on your studio, including how long you've been in business, outstanding features that make your studio unique. If you are to be the chief designer on the project, include a section on your years in business and any special awards or honors you have received. Too your own horn, but be succinct.

■ *Situation analysis*. Show that you understand the company's problems and areas of concern and how you can address them.

■ *Marketing analysis*. This section is used to demonstrate your understanding of the project's purpose. Convey your perception of the client's target market segment, and of how to approach it from a design point of view. Differentiate your design strategy from traditional approaches.

■ *Design requirements*. This is where you state your understanding of the job scope. This information is mostly available from the client. Does the design have to fit a certain space? Does it need to be mailed? Does it have to be printed in five different colors, or in a single trademarked color? Will it be used in many different sizes? List here the design parameters, and less obvious reasons why these parameters are "givens."

■ *Your design solution*. Here your words should accompany sketches or completed designs. Explain why you made certain design choices, listing both marketing and aesthetic reasons.

■ *Scheduling and cost analysis*. This section should contain a detailed budget, a payment schedule, and deadlines for the various stages of the design project. Be sure to detail the number of people from your studio who will be involved and their levels of expertise.

■ *Case studies*. List similar design projects you've done for other companies and their concrete results for those firms.

Unless it is absolutely unavoidable, you should never simply drop off a written proposal with your designs. It is very important

PROPOSAL TO ABC CORPORATION
IDENTITY SYSTEM

Phase I: Concept Exploration

We will develop an illustrative logo/icon representing each of your four product areas:

- Ice Cream
- Cookies
- Candy
- Frozen Yogurt

Based on our discussions, we will explore the concept of abstracted shapes of your products; for example, cones, circles, and swirled pyramids.

All four icons will be designed to be joined together to form the corporate signature for ABC Corporation.

The icons will be designed for individual use on packaging and point-of-sale materials, and for use as a unit on your letterhead and other corporate materials.

Our creative presentation to you will consist of the proposed art work, with variations showing alternative color schemes—ranging from the conservatively corporate to the more daring and contemporary.

We will also show—with full-sized color comps—how the design scheme will ultimately be applied to packaging, for example, on a yogurt carton and a candy wrapper.

Phase II: Logo Art and Stationery Production

Based on your input, we will refine the logo/icon designs and make final color and paper stock selections. We will prepare finished logo art and a master logo sheet for reproduction.

We will also produce mechanical art work for corporate letterhead, business cards, envelopes, and other stationery pieces or forms you may require.

At this time, we will work with you and the division heads to compile a list of the packaging and collateral materials to be designed, and will prepare a budget and schedule for implementation for those designs.

CORPORATE BROCHURE

Phase I: Comprehensive Presentation/ Storyboard

We will develop a brochure format that positions ABC Corporation as the leader and innovator in the sweet snacks and desserts industry.

The brochure will demonstrate to supermarket managers and other purchasing decision-makers that the ABC family of products will move off the shelves quickly and satisfy the sweet teeth of all of their customers.

To achieve this, the brochure can be based on a series of testimonials from kids, teenagers, moms and dads, and adult snackers. We will commission a series of black-and-white close-up portraits, each accompanied by a bold headline/quote. Each person's quote will highlight a different aspect of the satisfaction of eating and enjoying ABC products. We will also use small color still lifes to showcase the products.

Our presentation will consist of a full-sized cover design and one or two sample spreads showing proposed copy direction as well as visuals. They will be accompanied by a thumbnail storyboard showing the position of all elements in the brochure.

Phase II: Production

Upon your approval of the comp and storyboard, we will refine the design, select models, arrange for the photography, and supervise the shooting on location.

Working closely with your brand managers, we will write the copy, incorporating the facts determined by your research.

A complete, full-sized "dummy" of the brochure will be assembled, with all elements in position, for your approval.

Phase III: Mechanicals and Supervision

We will prepare camera-ready art work for twelve pages plus cover and supervise all aspects of pre- and on-press work, ensuring top quality and timely delivery of 5,000 brochures.

BUDGET: Fees for Professional Services
Identity System

Phase I: Design of four individual symbols/

icons which together form the corporate logotype. $0,000.
Phase II: Finished logo art and mechanicals for letterhead, envelope, business card. 0,000.

Corporate Brochure

For all phases as described in this proposal; to develop, write, art direct, and produce brochure; 12 pages plus cover. 00,000.

Estimated Out-of-Pocket Expenses

Portrait photography, three days on location, including assistant, film, processing, prints. 0,000.

Color product shots in studio. 0,000.

Models, props and location fees. 0,000.

Typesetting, approximately (for all pieces). 0,000.

Printing, 5,000 copies 16-page self-cover brochure on 60 lb. premium cover stock; 5 large duotone portraits, 5 minimum color separations, page size 9" × 12". 00,000.
Stats, retouching, and other miscellaneous expenses. 0,000.

Total $00,000.

Financial Information

Design fees are billed at the completion of each phase. We will require a $0,000 retainer (one-half of the Phase I fee) before beginning work, which will be applied to your final invoice.

Additional work not described in this proposal—including additional comps or presentations, additional pages, changes to approved layouts, and mechanical corrections (AAs)—is billed in addition to the quoted fee at hourly rates as follows:

Principal $000
Senior Designer/Production Manager $00
Design Assistant/Mechanical Artist $00

Out-of-pocket expenses are estimated in the proposal, and are billed upon completion of each respective phase at our actual costs plus the standard 17.65% agency commission.

If this proposal is agreeable to you, we will prepare an AIGA Agreement between client and designer, for your review and signature. We will begin work upon receipt of the Agreement and retainer.

I will be happy to answer any questions you may have about this Proposal/Estimate and the Agreement.

January 00, 1991

Eager Designers
789 Small Street
Our Town, USA
00000

Mr. Chief Executive Officer and President
ABC Corporation, Inc.
456 Major Avenue
Any Town, USA 00000

Dear Mr. Officer,

It is our pleasure to present this proposal for an identity system and a promotional brochure for ABC Corporation.

Our first priority will be to develop a graphic "look," including logo design and typography, that will give the company an appropriate, recognizable, and distinctive identity in the marketplace.

We will then design and produce a promotional brochure that will effectively demonstrate how ABC's products benefit its diverse customer base.

In the proposal you will find a description of the design and other work we propose to provide over the next three months, a budget, and information about the Eager Designers firm. When Phase I is completed, we will prepare a follow-up proposal describing the implementation of this graphic identity to all your product packaging.

Our cost estimates are contingent upon acceptance of the concepts described in this proposal, and are subject to change based on your further input.

I very much look forward to working with you and contributing to the "sweet success" of ABC.

Sincerely,

Eager Designer

Eager Designer
encl.

This example of a design proposal shows how a project should be broken into steps. The proposal should explain the steps involved and should give price estimates so the potential client can determine if the cost is in her ballpark. Also, use this opportunity to establish your terms up front.

that you present your design ideas *in person*. The text should be used to back up what you say and as a reference for project team members to look back on to clarify any points.

Don't model your verbal presentation on your written one. Your audience will become bored if you give the background they already know as a build up to presenting your designs. Instead, show your designs to everyone in the group, give them a few minutes to look at them carefully, and then begin answering questions or detailing the reasons for your choices of color, shape, type, and other elements. This is your chance to show your knowledge of the problem and the efficacy of your solution. Again, before you leave the meeting, make sure that either a decision has been reached or that a date has been agreed upon for when you will hear of their decision.

Presenting Additional Design Applications

You may include additional applications of your design in your verbal and written presentations as the last category to be considered, or the opportunity may arise to present these applications after your initial design idea has been accepted. In either case, suggesting additional design applications is usually a profitable idea. Since the initial design work is already done, coming up with additional applications provides an opportunity for you to earn more money from the original idea. Clients are usually delighted that you have gone to the trouble of considering other design applications and actually doing rough thumbnail sketches of the possibilities. Even if they don't end up buying the additional ideas, you'll have invested very little extra work for what can be a very profitable payoff.

Many designers find it helpful to have a brainstorming session with other studio members (or even with friends or family) to consider applications for the design other than those the client originally envisioned (see Joe Duffy's personal profile in this chapter). If the client asked for a letterhead and logo, you might suggest using the design on company give-aways as well (T-shirts, or pens, perhaps). If you're doing packaging, suggest that the design be used on point-of-display materials too. With a little marketing imagination, you can make your design ideas even more profitable for you and your client than either of you originally imagined.

DO YOU NEED A SALES REPRESENTATIVE?

While sales reps were once used mostly by photographers and illustrators, in an increasingly competitive design market, more and more designers are using them too. While the right sales rep can do wonders for your studio's bottom line, the wrong one can tarnish your reputation for years to come. So, you must be careful. The process of finding the right person isn't an easy one, so consider the following ideas for how to find the best rep for your studio.

■ Just as you do when considering any staffing matter for your studio, analyze your staffing needs and create a job description for your new sales rep. You may just want someone to handle the books, billing or pricing jobs. If so, then what you want is a business manager, not a sales rep. If you want someone to give you ideas about ways to market your designs and how to reach the right creative services buyers, then you need a marketing consultant. But if what you want is someone to represent you to clients and art directors, make cold calls and take inquiries, work on proposals, and even make presentations of your designs to clients, then what you want is a sales rep.

Decide exactly which tasks you want a sales rep to handle. For instance, are you happy to do initial meetings and client presentations, but terrified of cold calls and perplexed by mailing lists? Happy to peddle your portfolio but confused about contract negotiations? *Don't* let the sales rep decide who handles what—figure out what you'd like to handle and are good at, and hire someone who can take care of the rest.

■ Look for someone who has the capacity to understand your studio. In many ways, the sales rep position is the most crucial in your studio. Make sure that his personal style is consistent with your way of doing things, albeit slightly more aggressive on the marketing front. Since design is such a highly personal product, the personality of your sales rep matters a great deal. Be sure he understands both your design philosophy and the markets you work in. You are trusting this person with the promotion of your most valuable asset: your professional design reputation.

■ Draft a detailed contract that stipulates exactly how the sales rep will be compensated in various situations and what your activity and productivity expectations are. If you hire a sales rep on staff, he or she should get a modest base salary plus commissions. A freelance sales rep should get about 25 percent of the total fee for all jobs he brings in, with a slightly larger cut for out of town clients and slightly less for clients you may have both worked on snaring. You must also account for a sales rep's cut on things like sales of additional rights or uses, and issues such as who pays travel and entertainment expenses. The Graphic Artists Guild and the Society of Photographers and Artists Representatives (SPAR) have both drafted sample sales rep-artist contracts that you can use as guidelines. SPAR is also an excellent source of recommendations when you're looking for a sales rep. Contact them at 1123 Broadway, New York, NY 10010, 212-924-6023.

CHAPTER SEVEN
TROUBLESHOOTERS

Q. *The sales rep that I hired on a commission basis three months ago has been doing a great job getting clients for me so far. However, he recently negotiated a deal for my studio to design several print ads for a company that sells a service I disapprove of on moral grounds. I won't design for this firm, but my sales rep did his job. Do I owe him anything even though I didn't take the client he brought me?*

A. Check your contract with him. Many sales rep contracts contain a clause that stipulates that you may refuse a client, and in this case, the sales rep's commission is zero. The sales rep's commission is also zero if you never receive payment for the job, and if you only receive partial payment, the rep gets 25 percent of the total collected. If you value this rep, you might want to pay him a small amount for his time, especially if you did not specifically include the right to refuse a job in your contract with him. But make sure he has a better idea of what is and isn't acceptable to you from here on out.

Q. *In a recent client presentation, I was stopped cold by a rudely phrased question about a color choice I had made for a company logo. The questioner shot me down, and I stuttered and stammered out a half-baked defense. I know it made me look weak and uncertain, but I didn't want to just say nothing. What should I have done?*

A. Your first impulse was to duck and cover, but in most cases, it's better to stop a moment to think. Try not to react to the hostile phrasing of such questions. Instead, consider the content of the question, and formulate your answer and the reasoning behind it, focusing on logic rather than emotion. Take the extra time you need to ponder it carefully, in silence. And then give the answer matter-of-factly. This will show that solid reasoning underlies your design decisions, and that you are confident in the effectiveness of your work. An alternative would be to delicately probe his reason for asking. His response would give you two advantages: 1. You'll know what his real concerns are about the color (maybe the CEO hates red and has asked them to stay away from that color on all packages) and 2. Knowing the *real* area of concern gives you the opportunity to answer the *real* question, not just the question you were asked—often two different things.

Q. *During a client presentation, I mentioned a case study for a similar product that I had included in my written proposal. The marketing director said, "Oh, that irritating poster for XYZ—that was yours? It seemed like a jumble of type and color to me!" Since I had already included it in my written proposal, there was nothing I could do but smile wryly and say, "Yes, we did that." What do you do when something you thought was bragging backfires?*

A. You missed a golden opportunity by turning the focus away from the XYZ campaign. You should use case histories because they prove the *effectiveness* of a campaign, not necessarily because they are your most beautiful work (although often the two go together). A better answer would have been: "Too bad you didn't like those posters—I really enjoyed designing them. And XYZ enjoyed the 20 percent jump in sales they experienced after that campaign. Every company has its own way of looking at their products; XYZ may make sneakers similar to yours, but they wanted to represent them the way they're shown on this poster. The bottom line here is that I listen to my clients and come up with effective designs that represent their products and get results.

CHAPTER SEVEN
CHECKLISTS

In presenting portfolios:
- ☐ Combine different design pieces for each situation.
- ☐ Mount smaller pieces together.
- ☐ Use uniformly sized boards.
- ☐ Include only your best work.
- ☐ Enclose a studio brochure and business card.
- ☐ Note when to follow up on your presentation.

You will feel more secure in your speaking and writing skills if you:
- ☐ Make sure your grammar is impeccable.
- ☐ Prepare thoroughly.
- ☐ Don't rush through your presentation or proposal.
- ☐ Complete a first draft, then edit.
- ☐ Write to express, not to impress.
- ☐ Avoid tentative or passive language.
- ☐ Make sure there are not typographical errors in your proposal.
- ☐ Don't obsess about small mistakes.

When making cold telephone calls:
- ☐ State immediately why you are calling.
- ☐ Be clear and concise.
- ☐ Mention any mutual acquaintance or other connection.
- ☐ Be persistent but not obnoxious.

When you drop off a portfolio:
- ☐ Dress neatly even if you don't plan to meet with the creative services buyer.
- ☐ Come prepared with questions about the firm and its design needs.
- ☐ Ask when you should expect an answer or plan to recontact.

For the initial project meeting:
- ☐ Consider it as important as the design presentation.
- ☐ Prepare by learning all you can about the company from outside sources.
- ☐ Use the meeting to ask questions about the company, market, product, etc.
- ☐ Get a sense of the power structure within the company.
- ☐ Leave with a commitment about what the next action step will be.

For the design presentation:
- ☐ Prepare a written proposal including:
  - Introduction.
  - Company background.
  - Situation analysis.
  - Market analysis.
  - Design requirements.
  - Your design solution.
  - Scheduling and cost analysis.
  - Case studies.
- ☐ Verbally present your designs first, then back up design decisions with marketing facts in your written proposal.

Consider presenting additional design applications:
- ☐ Brainstorm first to come up with varied design applications.
- ☐ Additional applications show your interest in the company.
- ☐ Additional applications cost your studio relatively little for a potentially profitable payoff.

If you are considering hiring a sales representative:
- ☐ Figure out if a sales rep is really what you need.
- ☐ Prepare a detailed job description.

CHAPTER 8
MANAGING YOUR STAFF EFFECTIVELY

PROFIT POINTS

Build a solid team by:

- Knowing when you need extra help.
- Using hiring methods that guarantee you'll get the right people.
- Letting your staff know when they're on (and off) track.
- Setting clear, achievable goals for meaningful progress.
- Setting salaries that won't break the budget.
- Knowing when letting someone go is in your best interest.

The most important resource a design firm has is its employees. In the design business, the people who work for you *are* your business, pure and simple. That is why carefully staffing and managing your studio has a direct impact on how profitable it is. Even if the other people in your studio are support staff and only you create the designs you sell, your studio's profits depend on smooth teamwork and on the atmosphere the blend of personalities creates.

This chapter will stress the importance of staff management, building a team environment in your studio, and handling the administrative staff management needs of your firm, such as employee reviews, hiring and firing.

Before you think about hiring any employee or adding freelancers, you need to critically analyze the current tasks and responsibilities that you expect staff members in your studio to perform. The simplest way to do this is to write out a valid job description for everyone in your studio, including yourself.

HOW TO WRITE A JOB DESCRIPTION

A job description is a concise, exact description of job responsibilities, desirable traits of the job holder, and possibilities for training and advancement. The job description should serve as a document to establish expectations: what you expect from an employee and what a job candidate can expect from you. Job descriptions should be written for both your own employees and for freelancers. John H. Melchinger, publisher of a newsletter for small businesses called *Minding Your Own Business*, published by the John H. Melchinger Co., suggests the following guidelines for writing a job description:

1. State the job title, to whom the person reports, and the primary duties and responsibilities of the position.
2. Specify the knowledge, skills, educational background, or work experience required to do the job well.
3. List the personal characteristics that will enable someone to do this job well. Mention things like attention to detail, efficiency, stamina, and good writing or people skills.
4. Describe what job opportunities will be available to the person who performs this job well. If there is a path for advancement, make that clear. Also mention the training you are willing to provide for a person in this position who would like to advance.

Job descriptions are not trivial formalities. It is important that you take the time necessary to do them well. Consider the hours you will put into interviewing and evaluating candidates and training the one you choose. Poor communication at the beginning of the hiring process leads to a high turnover rate, which can cost your company thousands of dollars in lost work hours, training time, and unemployment insurance. The hours you invest upfront will add to your studio's profits by insuring you fill positions with just the right people. Job descriptions provide an accurate basis for staffing since you are focusing on tasks and responsibilities, not job titles or categories.

Before deciding whether you need to expand your staff, and in which areas, analyze all of the tasks each member of your staff is responsible for. What does each staff member spend most of his time doing? Are some people performing tasks that are beneath their skill levels? (Remember, you are paying them for what they are capable of doing, and if you're not using their skills to the fullest, you're losing big dollars.) Are people working less productively on tasks they hate? Can work be reassigned to even out project assignments and tasks and thus make more efficient use of your staff?

Do you spend hours doing simple production chores that you could be paying someone else to do? Never forget the value of your own time and the impact your own billing has on your profits. Remember that even if you don't subtract an hourly wage from your studio's profits for your own time, an hour of designer's time is worth much more than the same hour for a production artist. If you're doing menial tasks instead of designing, you are costing your business money.

HOW TO HIRE

Once you've decided, based on your analysis, that your studio needs to expand, you must decide whether you want to hire a person on a freelance, contractual basis or as a full-time or part-time employee. There are tax and business advantages to each. Although you should discuss these advantages with your accountant or attorney, there is one guideline: If your studio's workflow tends to be cyclical, you may be better off hiring people on a freelance basis. With freelance help, when work is slow, you're not stuck with a non-productive employee, their salary, and no income to justify the headcount. But remember, with freelancers, that freedom goes both ways—if someone offers them more money or more enjoyable work, you could be stuck looking for a new person right in the middle of your busiest season.

The advantage to hiring other designers on staff (rather than as freelancers) is that when you find the right people, your studio will begin to develop a "look" that is a combination of all your designers' best work. If a client doesn't like one person's designs, he may like another's, and you'll have a better chance of attracting a wider variety of clients.

There is one more step you need to do before you begin your employee search. You have to set a salary range for the position.

Setting a Salary

To find out what people make, read other want ads, call placement agencies specializing in creative positions, and check with colleagues. Once you have a ballpark salary figure, take into consideration the specific candidate to whom you would most like to offer the job. Experience in a similar position adds to the salary a person can command, as does a high level of specialized education and unique skills. Factor all of these things in when making someone an offer.

In general, you will more than make the money back if you offer a salary slightly higher than the going rate. If you try to get a good employee at a cheap price, that person will eventually end up resenting you and the studio for taking advantage of her and may well make up the salary difference by performing poorly on the job. As one New York City designer puts it, "If you pay someone like a jerk, and treat him like a jerk—guess what? He acts like a jerk. But, if you compensate someone well and give him the respect a valued member of your studio deserves, then guess what? He'll act like a professional, valuable member of your studio, whether he is an administrative assistant or a senior designer. Pay people what they're worth, and most will be worth far more to your studio than you could ever pay them."

Company Benefits

To set a competitive salary, you have to consider company benefits as well. Most employees factor the cost and value of company benefits into their salaries; a prudent employer should do the same. Depending on the size of your studio, there are a variety of benefits you may want to offer employees. However, the cost of these benefits, especially health insurance, has skyrocketed over the last few years, so be sure your company can afford a benefits package on a long-term basis before committing to one. You should discuss your benefits package with your accountant or attorney with regard to its financial practicality, and any legal requirements for employers in your state.

Some of the benefits your studio might offer are:

- Health insurance (Either traditional coverage with a deductible or a health maintenance organization [HMO]. Some states require that health insurance be provided to all employees, so check with your accountant or attorney about

this point.).
- Paid vacation.
- Life insurance.
- Disability insurance.
- A retirement savings plan (often with matching company contributions).
- A profit sharing plan offering stock in the company or cash bonuses.
- Various small benefits (parking, health club membership, day care, matching charitable contributions, time off, free snacks or soft drinks at work).

Another reason to offer group benefits is that you can take advantage of them yourself. Having a company plan at your studio may save you a bundle on your own personal health, life and disability insurance costs.

Keep in mind that freelancers and independent contractors usually don't get company benefits, which is why their hourly pay may be higher than that of the people on staff.

Now you're ready to look for that perfect job applicant. Interviewing and hiring the right people is an art in itself, but it is something that you can learn. The following sections will provide you with guidelines for reviewing résumés and portfolios and interviewing candidates to insure you choose the right person for the job every time.

Résumés

You should require a resume from all applicants, from designers to receptionists, freelancers to potential staff employees. A résumé provides important information about the candidate that portfolios and interviews cannot convey. Here are some ideas on what to look for in a résumé and what it can tell you about the person:

- High levels of achievement in a focused direction.
- Specific, action-oriented descriptions of job responsibilities. Look for verbs like "managed," "designed," or "executed," rather than "assisted with" or "reported to." This will tell you the level of responsibility and the real

PERSONAL PROFILE

DICK MITCHELL
Richards Brock Miller Mitchell and Associates
Dallas, Texas

"I'm a great believer in the jack-of-all-trades method of running a design studio," says Dick Mitchell, design partner in the Dallas design firm of Richards Brock Miller Mitchell and Associates. "Our studio has thirteen designers who do it all—design, write, illustrate, handle production work and press runs, and even act as studio reps. Being able to follow a design idea from the beginning sketches to the final press run offers most of our people a great sense of accomplishment."

So how does Richards Brock et al. find such talented jacks- and jills-of-all-trades? By hiring with an eye toward the future, says Mitchell. Job candidates are told very clearly during the interview process what the studio wants from them, both now and down the road, and what their future with the company could be like. Possible hires are questioned very closely about their own ambitions, because the studio believes strongly that employees who set their goals high and work toward them can't help but bring the studio along in their climb to success.

"Because our designers are so good, they often get offers from other studios. From the day we hire a designer, we encourage her to be very honest with us about her satisfaction at work, and to talk with us openly if she gets another offer and is seriously considering it.

"Besides open discussion and a future with the studio, we also keep talented people by paying them well. In general, we pay as much as we can in annual salary, plus we have profit sharing and yearly bonus plans for all employees. Although money isn't everything, it is a good way to show people the fruits of their hard work. And having some part of compensation based on the studio's profits makes everyone well aware of whether last year was up or down for the studio financially. It also gives people a real stake in the work they do every day," observes Mitchell.

tasks that the candidate performed.

■ Orientation toward profit—look for candidates (both designers *and* support people) who state how their work quantitatively helped the company's bottom line. If they have a reputation for watching costs, creatively saving a company money on a project, they'll do the same for you.

■ Stable, consistent upward direction shown in a series of job advancements within the field (rather than *lateral* hopping from company to company). A "job hopper" may be incompetent, or just restless—either trait won't be a plus for your studio.

■ Excellent educational qualifications and awards.

■ A coherent, organized resume format without too much "flash." Be aware that in the design field many people may use their resume to show off their design skills. Be wary of glitzy candidates who may have no substance.

Divide candidates into three groups based on their résumés alone: to interview, maybe and no way. Send the "no ways" a polite rejection letter and keep their résumés on file. Interview all of the "yes" group and at least a few of the "maybes." Keep track of which category you tend to hire from; if you're hiring maybes on a regular basis, you probably need to sharpen your résumé-evaluation skills.

Judging the Portfolio

There are probably as many criteria for judging a portfolio as there are design styles. But, besides relying on your own instinctive feelings when judging a body of work, you should look for:

■ Problem solving rather than "decorating."
■ Diversity of design and application of ideas.
■ A style that is a "signature," not a clone.
■ Immaculate execution of designs, showing attention not only to the art but also the craft of design.

It also helps to have at least one other de-signer (preferably someone with a very different design sense than yours, but whose work you admire) look over the best portfolios. If she likes some of the same designs you do, then you can be more confident that they stand out because they are smart designs, not just eye-catching artwork.

The Interview

Most people fall into one of two categories: those who readily sing their praises and those who have a difficult time talking about themselves. Designers are visual people and have a tendency to express themselves more comfortably through their work than verbally in an interview setting. You don't have to fill the silence. Your job is to let the candidate sell himself before you sell him on your company. Do more listening than talking, even if the job candidate is the quiet type.

To get a deeper understanding of a candidate, try provocative questions such as:

■ *"What were the five most important duties in your last position and how did you perform them?"* (This reveals a person's grasp of both the function and the process of a job. Also, if he mentions a duty and then can't adequately explain how he performed it, he may be exaggerating his experience.)

■ *"Describe the best boss you ever had."* (You'll learn what the job candidate needs and values from an employer.)

■ *"What do you do when a problem has really got you stumped?"* (This answer will indicate how independently the candidate works and whether the person is a flexible thinker and a competent problem-solver. This will also tell you how she deals with the typical frustrations a designer faces, such as dealing with creative blocks.

■ *"What risks did you take in your last job, and what happened?"* (This lets you know if the candidate is a self-starter, what he considers a "risk," and how confident he is in his own abilities.)

■ *"What have been your biggest frustrations and failures?"* (You can gauge a candidate's self-knowledge and honesty with this question.)

■ *"How did you make your last employer's investment in you pay off?"* (The right answer can show loyalty and attention to an employer's profitability.)

■ *"How could your present company be run better?"* (If he is full of ideas and suggestions rather than complaints and criticism, he might be a great asset to your studio. If he says, "I don't know," or proceeds to concentrate on bad-mouthing his present company, steer clear of this one. He isn't concerned with your business, only his own paycheck.

BUILDING A WINNING TEAM

One key requirement of building a profitable staff at your firm is to develop a group of people who work effectively as a team. Some projects might be successfully handled by a single employee, but the studio staff needs to function as a team for projects to be completed efficiently and well. If team members compete unproductively among themselves, each trying to thwart the others' efforts, projects will flounder. Meanwhile, you're paying salaries, but nothing is being accomplished. Such "down time" is not billable time; therefore, you're losing money if there is a weak, resistant or overly competitive member on your team.

To Help a Team Work Efficiently:

■ First, work with individual team members to set goals and deadlines. Discuss expectations and deadlines for projects, decision-making authority, and lines of communication (who to consult with problems, who she should report to, and who should be reporting to her). Again, consensus helps ensure cooperation.

■ Solicit team members' help in planning and estimating your project schedule. Individual members know how they work and it is only fair for them to establish what they feel is an appropriate deadline for various stages of

PERSONAL PROFILE

DON TROUSDELL
Trousdell Design
Atlanta, Georgia

"I still think that design should be a cottage industry," says Don Trousdell, owner of Trousdell Design, a studio in Atlanta that specializes in advertising design. "When a studio stays small and simple, it's lighter on its feet. It can change according to each client's needs and keep up with new design styles as well."

Trousdell practices what he preaches. With a staff of only seven people (two other designers besides Trousdell, one production artist, one rep/production person, one purely rep person, and a bookkeeper), Trousdell Design handles such plum clients as Customweave Carpets and Kimberly-Clark. Although Trousdell hasn't taken on a new staff member in several years, he still looks at countless portfolios each month and has a unique method of judging which designers have that extra spark needed to turn a good studio into a design leader. He advises, "Look for designs that are intelligent, that show an ability to solve communication or image problems, and not just 'pretty' things up. I also analyze how the design itself is put together—is this designer a careful artisan as well as an inventive thinker?

"Extending an idea to different design applications is an important source of profits, especially in advertising design. When I look at a portfolio, I ask myself: Has the artist extended her design idea to other areas of ad design, such as packaging or field support materials? Not only is this a good sign of creativity in a portfolio, it also shows attention to the studio's financial well-being, since different applications of the same design idea mean more income for the studio.

"In general," Trousdell notes, "I look for someone who handles a design problem completely differently than I would have—and does it better."

the project. A major advantage to including team members in your planning is that by including staff at the beginning of a project, they become more responsible and accountable for their work. They assume "ownership" of the project, and thus want to do a great job.

■ Don't dictate—facilitate. Encourage employee independence and creative problem-solving abilities in your staff.

■ Don't gloss over problems in the way the team functions. If there is a glitch or a conflict, sit down with the whole team, pinpoint the problem, and work out a solution.

■ Encourage everyone to enjoy their creativity, but remind them that cost control is as important an issue as creative design work. Team members should be aware of how mistakes in the project cost the studio money.

HOW TO MANAGE YOUR STAFF EFFECTIVELY

Design work is an intensively people-oriented type of business. For this reason, how well you manage your staff will be a major factor in determining how profitably and happily your studio operates.

We've discussed the need to establish a team atmosphere in your studio. Make it clear from the first day that you have chosen your new employee because you feel that she can benefit from working for the company, and the entire company can benefit from having her aboard. People who truly feel they belong and are needed do their best to perform for the team. A maximum effort translates directly into maximized profits.

Follow these guidelines to motivate your employees to do their best:

■ Set standards for your studio, your employees and yourself. Communicate these standards through words and your actions, and make it clear that you expect the best from everyone. In rising to the challenge, people will do great work—for the studio and for their own satisfaction.

■ Set the tone for open communication. Be honest and straightforward with people about your own mistakes. Encourage people to come to you with theirs. The only thing that can hurt a studio more than a bad mistake is the wasted effort (and, ultimately, money in lost billing time) that may be expended trying to cover it up. Trust your people and make it clear that they can trust you.

■ Foster independence in your employees. One way you can do this is to expect your staff to take the initiative and be innovative. The whole studio will run more effectively and profitably if you can concentrate on your own work and don't have to waste time hand-holding. Any number of heads *is* better than one—look for new ideas from all your people. Recognize good ideas and don't penalize or ridicule employees for bad ones.

■ Always give both public and private praise for a job well done. Back up your words with small bonuses: cash, lunch, flowers, theater tickets, or even a simple pat on the back. A small token of appreciation can be very meaningful to people. Invest everyone in the studio's "big picture." Consult all levels of employees on future plans, and give news and copies of the studio's quarterly earnings to everyone. Let people see exactly what kind of impact their efforts have on the studio as a whole, and get them involved and invested in running the company well from whichever level they work.

There are two other duties of staff management and administration that are considered necessary evils: periodic staff reviews and employee dismissal. These are both important areas of staffing that can have a direct negative impact on your bottom line if too little attention is paid to them. Marginal employees who receive a helpful employee review can become much more productive if steered in the right direction; if they don't, unfortunately, you may have to let them go.

HOW TO REVIEW YOUR STAFF'S PERFORMANCE

Designers are in a different category than most "mainstream" professionals. The work they produce is a direct reflection of their personalities and their creativity. Although it can be very difficult to offer and to accept criticism, performance reviews are necessary for the productivity and profitability of your studio. It is essential that you point out to your employees what it is they are doing right *and* what could be improved.

Employees should be reviewed after their first three months at your studio, followed by regularly scheduled reviews at six-month intervals. The following guidelines will help you conduct more effective and productive employee reviews:

■ Make up a standard form to use for all performance reviews. List the person's different job responsibilities (you should review the person's job description to make sure you have taken all job responsibilities into account) and rate her performance of each task on a one to five scale. Along with job-specific duties, include behaviors that contribute to the well-being of the studio as a whole and that apply to all employees such as attendance, working well with the team, attentiveness to company goals (including profitability), general creativity, and companywide initiative.

■ One week before the scheduled interview, give an employee a blank performance review form to fill out. This will provide you with an idea of how the employee views herself. You might expect employees to rate themselves as perfect, but you will be surprised at the honesty with which they evaluate themselves.

■ Give the employee a copy of your written evaluation at the end of the workday before the day of your scheduled meeting. This gives the employee overnight to think about the evaluation and prepare for the meeting.

■ Schedule an uninterrupted half-hour or so to talk over the review. This shows that you take the person and his development as a valued member of the studio team very seriously.

■ Use specific examples in both praise and criticism of a person's performance. In other words, don't say, "You're irresponsible," but instead say, "When you missed the printer's deadline for the Martinson job, you delayed the whole project and cost this studio X number of work hours and X dollars."

■ Deliver negative criticism in a frank but positive way. Never criticize a behavior without reiterating the way you would have preferred things to be handled. Even if you're exasperated by the person's apparent inability to change, stress and re-stress what you'd like to see happen.

■ Let the employee reply. However, don't put him on the defensive, eliciting excuses. Cut long-winded explanations short politely, and say "Let's not focus on what went wrong; let's talk about how we're going to work together to make it right. What are your ideas?"

■ Set specific goals. If vaguely stated, objectives won't help improve performance. You shouldn't impose your own goals, however, but work with the person to set goals you both agree on. Mutually conceived goals are more readily accepted by employees than ones you might try to formulate alone.

■ Don't focus on personality, unless a person's demeanor is harming her ability to get the job done or hurting the entire team. Focus instead on what needs to be done, and how this employee could better accomplish those tasks.

In general, it's best to think of yourself as a coach in performance reviews. What you want is to build a winning team, not cut people down. Make them well aware of both their shortcomings and their talents, and then focus on improvement and support. If a performance review deteriorates into a scolding, you are wasting everyone's time.

Most annual performance reviews involve salary increases. Be prepared to consider what the individual is worth in terms of the current market value. Have the cost of living, the economy or salary differentials changed dramatically since the employee's last salary increase? Have her duties and responsibilities changed?

If positive changes don't come about after you've given a formal employee review, and a reasonable amount of time has passed to allow for the change to begin appearing, you may have to fire the employee.

HOW TO FIRE SOMEONE

Firing one of your studio's members is never pleasant. But to handle the dismissal fairly and assure your own peace of mind, you must remember that firing someone is a business decision, and you must treat it as such. The following tips can help you handle an uncomfortable, but sometimes unavoidable situation:

■ *Give fair warning.* As soon as you notice that an employee is not performing well, sit down with him and discuss the problem(s) at length. Give suggestions for improvement and set a reasonable time frame in which you expect the person to turn his performance around. Generally one month for improvement and several months thereafter to watch for consistency in the improvement should be adequate. If the situation persists, document the problem consistently through the use of formal performance reviews. In your meetings, ask the employee if he has any suggestions for how his performance can be improved. You'll be surprised at the honesty you'll receive and the creative and generally positive suggestions a troublesome employee may offer to help turn the situation around.

■ *Set a probation period.* If the person doesn't seem able to make a change for the better, write a memo that reiterates the content of the "fair warning" talk, and set a deadline by which either you expect to see substantial improvement or the person will be dismissed. Give the employee two copies of the memo, asking that he keep a copy and return a copy to you with his signature.

■ *Keep an accurate employee file.* You must be able to show substantial reason for dismissal, in case you are sued for wrongful discharge or age, gender or race discrimination. If you think that you may have to fire an employee, be sure to keep copies of all performance reviews, warning memos, and even examples of poorly performed work.

■ *Fire the person quietly and alone.* Don't get into a discussion of his merits or shortcomings. Nor should you entertain a litany of excuses or accusations. Just explain matter-of-factly that the studio no longer can afford his services. It is a business decision. Be firm, not cruel. If a person gets angry or cries, let him express his emotions briefly, but then get back to the business at hand — severing the business relationship between the employee and your studio. *Never* yell "You're fired!" at someone in a moment of anger — if you end up reversing your decision, you'll never be taken seriously again.

■ *Have all the paperwork in front of you.* Give the dismissed person a packet with his severance check (if you do pay severance — it is not required by law), a check to cover unused vacation days or other compensation, and insurance transfer forms. That way, the former employee can't barter for extra severance or "just one more chance."

■ *Be sympathetic.* Express your honest regret that the studio could not use this person's talents effectively. It will help both of you not to "burn bridges." Think of the problem between the studio and the fired employee as a bad fit instead of blaming the person for his own downfall. After all, in most communities the design field is fairly small, and you never know when you may have to work with this person again in another capacity.

CHAPTER EIGHT
TROUBLESHOOTERS

Q. *I run a small studio with three other designers besides myself. Two of the other designers are great, but the third is a real terror. She is nasty, argumentative and bullying, but everyone agrees that her designs are terrific. Is there any way to make life more pleasant around our studio?*

A. There are two rules of thumb that may help in dealing with such an ornery character: Don't take it personally, and hold your own without engaging in a power struggle. It's easy to find yourself fighting with such a person over nothing, just because when you're kicked you want to kick back.

Instead, ask yourself: 1. If the issue is worth fighting over, or 2. Whether you have the power to handle it without involving her. If the issue is not important enough for this kind of friction, don't fight for the sake of fighting—just back down. And if you can handle it without her OK, just cut her tirade short with something like "That's enough. I'm well aware of your opinion on this. I have no need to discuss this further with you."

Above all, maintain your own calm and self-respect. If you do need her cooperation or agreement for something and she is screaming at you, simply walk away, and tell her you'll return to discuss it when you both can do so in a business-like manner. If she's left yelling at an empty room often enough, she'll clue in to the fact that she had better find a more constructive way to deliver her opinions.

Q. *Recently, our studio lost a huge client, and, in the same week, our production artist was killed in an auto accident. Morale hit rock bottom and has stayed there ever since. What can I do?*

A. Firings, deaths or illnesses, or even losing an important client can send studio morale into a tailspin. The most crucial aspect of handling employee morale problems is to acknowledge them. Don't try to gloss over the problem with corporate cheerleading. Instead, call an all-studio meeting and encourage everyone to voice their feelings and fears. Just listen, and share a few of your own doubts. Focus on the support you can give each other and your hopes of mending the problem. Again, enlist everyone's input on how to improve the situation. And after the meeting is over, follow it up with other discussions and frequent progress reports. Instead of letting people remain isolated in their separate slumps, point everyone toward the company goals you all share and fire them up by giving them the power and strategies to overcome the negatives.

Q. *One of our junior designers is a classic underachiever. Every once in a while, he comes up with some great work in a burst of glory, but most of the time he does mediocre designs. How can I get him to shine more often?*

A. Poor performers usually need a combination of three things: special attention, higher standards, and targets to shoot for. If you feel this person is both willing and capable of being salvaged, then it is probably worth the effort to try. Show a sincere, personal interest in his work, and let him know that you believe he is capable of doing better. Use his own designs as proof of his talent. Ask him what he expects from himself, and let him know that your expectations are even higher. Give him something to stretch toward. Finally, work with him to set specific goals for his work. Many people only need an initial, supportive push to get rolling. Then their new self-confidence feeds their success, which in turn reinforces their self-confidence further and feeds more success.

CHAPTER EIGHT
CHECKLISTS

Before hiring:
- ☐ Analyze your studio's personnel budget.
- ☐ Make sure staff members are not doing tasks below their skill-level.
- ☐ Write a job description for the position you've created.
- ☐ Hire someone to handle tasks that take you away from creative and billable design work.
- ☐ Decide whether to make the job you're hiring for a freelance or staff position.

When writing a job description, include:
- ☐ Job title.
- ☐ Supervisor.
- ☐ Primary duties and responsibilities.
- ☐ Education and skills required.
- ☐ Desirable personal characteristics for this position.
- ☐ Possibilities for advancement.

When reading résumés look for:
- ☐ Focused, consistent achievements.
- ☐ Specific descriptions of duties performed.
- ☐ Awareness of and orientation toward profit making.
- ☐ Stable, upward career moves rather than lateral job-hopping.
- ☐ Educational achievements and other awards.
- ☐ A coherent, organized résumé format.

Look for these points when judging a portfolio:
- ☐ Immaculate execution of designs.
- ☐ Problem-solving rather than 'decorating.'
- ☐ Design diversity.
- ☐ Varied applications for the same design.

When conducting an interview:
- ☐ Listen rather than talk.
- ☐ Ask open-ended questions.
- ☐ Urge candidates to expand upon résumé information.

When setting a salary and establishing benefits:
- ☐ Set a salary slightly higher than average for your city.
- ☐ Possible benefit options:
    - Health insurance.
    - Paid vacation.
    - Life insurance.
    - Disability insurance.
    - Pension plan.
    - Profit sharing or bonuses.
    - Small perks, such as parking or health club memberships.

In building a winning team:
- ☐ Enlist the team's help in planning the project.
- ☐ Set goals, ground rules and deadlines by consensus.
- ☐ Don't ignore problems—work them out with the whole team.
- ☐ Facilitate, don't dictate.
- ☐ Focus everyone on cost control.

How to manage your staff profitably:
- ☐ Make each staff member feel a part of the studio.
- ☐ Set high standards for your staff and yourself.
- ☐ Require people to approach their jobs creatively.
- ☐ Let each person see his impact on company earnings.
- ☐ Foster independence.
- ☐ Create an environment of open communication.
- ☐ Praise people publicly and privately.

When conducting employee performance reviews:
- ☐ Schedule the reviews on a regular basis.
- ☐ Develop a standard review form with room to add specifics.
- ☐ Let the employee have input.
- ☐ Give the employee the evaluation to read before your meeting.
- ☐ Provide specific examples to back up your criticism.
- ☐ Deliver negatives frankly but optimistically.
- ☐ Let the person respond.
- ☐ Set goals for improvement.
- ☐ Don't evaluate personality flaws.

How to fire an employee:
- ☐ Give fair warning.
- ☐ Set a probation period.
- ☐ Keep an accurate, *documented* employee file.
- ☐ Fire the person quietly and alone.
- ☐ Have checks, insurance forms and other documents ready.
- ☐ Be sympathetic but matter-of-fact.

CHAPTER 9

USING PROFESSIONAL SERVICES WISELY

PROFIT POINTS

Save yourself thousands of dollars in mistakes *not made* by:

- Getting legal advice upfront.
- Finding accountants and tax planners to manage your finances.
- Hiring a bookkeeper.
- Knowing where to find answers to special business problems.

When you run your own studio, one of the hardest things to admit may be that you can't "do it all." The fact is, even if you do have the skills to both design a new corporate identity for a client *and* prepare your quarterly tax payments in the same work week, your primary duty is design. Spending extensive time and energy on other business chores will end up costing your business profits because you won't be billing anyone for your time.

This is not to say that you shouldn't be involved in running the business end of your studio. But one key to running a successful studio is knowing whom to hire—both on staff and as consultants—to help you handle the legal, financial and tax aspects of your business. (See Chapter Eight on staffing.)

In order to determine what kinds of professional help you'll need, take a long, hard look first at your own skills and talents, then at the size and nature of your business (or the business you're planning to start). Ideally, you should do this kind of analysis even before making the first move to set up your own studio. But it's never too late to start becoming more financially responsible, so if your studio is up and running, look at your business as it now operates.

Most smaller studios need a lawyer, someone to keep the books, and an accountant to help with tax preparation. In addition to these people, many studios hire outside consultants to help with such things as copywriting, finding a new studio space, planning the design of the workspace or overseeing renovations, choosing a benefits plan, pricing jobs, or making hiring decisions.

If you are just starting up a studio, you should look first for an attorney who specializes in handling small businesses. He or she can help guide your decisions from your first inkling that you may want to strike out on your own. A good small business lawyer can also advise you on how to find an accountant,which bank to approach for loans, how to set up a partnership, and other decisions crucial to getting your studio up and running. It is important to know both the questions to ask and the appropriate answers you are looking for.

GET THE RIGHT LEGAL ADVICE UPFRONT

Even if your studio is a one-person operation, you should have some kind of legal counsel. The time to look for an attorney is not when you hit a legal snag but before you really need him. It is best to develop a relationship with a lawyer from the time your studio opens for business. Send him contracts, lease agreements, or other documents you have questions about, use him to help draft your standard contracts, and make sure he is at least acquainted with your business *before* the first time you need to call on him for advice. Sound advice on planning and fiscal responsibility can save you thousands of dollars.

To come up with a list of potential attorneys to interview, consult colleagues who have gone into business for themselves. Even if you don't know many designers with their own studios, call the ones in your town and ask them who they use to handle legal matters. You'll be better off if you can find someone who not only understands the law, but also works with designers and other creative businesses and understands the special legal circumstances of selling a creative product.

Another source of prospective lawyers for your studio is your local Small Business Administration (SBA) office. If there is no SBA listing in your telephone book, call the national office in Washington, D.C. (see Resources list on page 130 for telephone number) and ask for a list of attorneys in your area that specialize in small business matters.

When you've developed a list of four or five candidates, call each to make an appointment for a first consultation. The cost of these first meetings can be steep ($100 to $250 an hour), but this expense can keep you from making the costlier mistake of hiring the wrong attorney.

WHAT TO ASK AN ATTORNEY

If you are seeking an attorney, here are some questions to ask to see if the attorney fits your needs:

Who will be handling my legal work? Although associates may prepare documents or do research, the only person who should represent you or counsel you is the attorney you hire. Make sure your business won't get shoved onto the back burner in favor of larger clients. If associates will be handling most of your legal matters, ask to see what their qualifications are. Often competent associates can end up saving you tremendous legal fees while providing excellent service.

What type of clients do you handle, how many, and of what size? Look for someone who represents businesses much like yours. You're paying for an attorney's experience, and the more businesses like yours he has handled, the more valuable his experience is to your business.

What is your workload like? Although it may seem that a popular attorney must necessarily be a good one, think again. An attorney who is constantly overworked or "very busy" may not be able to handle your problems with the speed or thoroughness that you'd like.

How can you help my particular busi- ness? Different studios need attorneys for different purposes. Does the one you're interviewing have the special skills your business requires? Expertise in setting up partnerships? A special knowledge of copyright laws? The ability to handle sticky tax situations? What about drawing up airtight contracts? Look for someone who is interested and experienced in the specialties you'll need him for.

Can you explain to me why you would advise certain legal actions? If an attorney either can't or won't explain the reasons behind his recommendations, then he is not for you. It is imperative that you understand and consent to any action your lawyer takes on your behalf, because you are ultimately responsible, both legally and financially, for its outcome. Find someone who is willing and able to explain his recommendations in terms you can understand.

What are your fees and how are they charged? You should expect regular, detailed bill, listing all charges. An attorney's time should be billed at an agreed hourly rate. If the attorney you choose asks for a retainer (a sum paid up front before you are taken on as a client, from which fees and expenses are deducted when work starts on your case), make sure that the contract you sign for his services ensures the return of the remainder of the retainer if you decide to fire him.

From your first contact with a lawyer, keep careful notes. Are your calls returned with reasonable promptness? Does the attorney seem to spend most of the work day in his office, where she can be easily reached? Is she polite, interested, clear and helpful over the telephone? It won't matter for your purposes how smart or esteemed an attorney is if you can't reach or communicate effectively with her.

Go to the first meeting with a list of questions for the attorney (see above), and a written profile of your studio or the one you plan to start. Describe your clients, your principal area of design, any other areas you dabble in or plan to enter to attract future clients, the equipment you own or plan to buy, and your studio's current bank loans or other debt. Provide copies of your quarterly tax returns and accounting statements for the last few years and your business plan (see Chapter One for details on how to write a business plan). You may want to send over the information a few days in advance of the consultation to give the lawyer a chance to look at the information about your studio before your meet. But be aware you may be charged for the time it takes him to read the material in addition to your consultation charge.

USING PROFESSIONAL SERVICES WISELY **121**

If you are lucky enough to find a great small business attorney, she may very well also lead you to the right accountant, banker, bookkeeper, business manager and consultants. In any case, you'll probably need to hire one or all of these people at some point or another. Following are some guidelines for spotting the best people in each field.

In making your choice, keep in mind the time-worn adage "An ounce of prevention is worth a pound of cure." Investing time and effort to find the right person can save you the anguish and money it could cost you to rectify a legal or financial nightmare caused by inept handling of your affairs. Your ultimate goal is to hire people you trust to act in your best interests so that you can devote yourself to the creative end of the business and building its profits.

HIRING ACCOUNTANTS AND TAX PLANNERS WHO CAN BUILD YOUR FINANCIAL PROFILE

The smaller your studio, the more important it is to choose an accountant with whom you can trust *all* of your financial information—both business and personal. Even if your studio is incorporated, your personal finances and the studio's business are necessarily intertwined, at least for tax and accounting purposes. If you feel you must keep financial secrets from your accountant, he simply won't be able to do the best job possible.

Most small studios use an accountant to set up an accounting system, train the owners or business manager to use it, and check the books quarterly (usually at the same time he prepares your quarterly estimated tax payments). Especially when you are starting out, an accountant's expertise in setting up a system to track your studio's funds can be invaluable. Once that system is in place and as long as it meets your business's needs, you should be able to keep track of payables and receivables in a fairly simple manner. If the system your accountant sets up isn't working for you, then have him revise it. Remember—it is the accountant's job to make things easier and

more workable for your studio, not the other way around.

Unless you have a particularly complicated tax situation, you'll probably be better off hiring an accountant who will also handle your taxes. Bringing in a separate tax planner at tax time just means that someone else will have to go over the accounting figures and reinterpret them. This leaves more room for simple errors that can muddle your books *and* your tax return, and even a casual mistake on a tax return can target you for an IRS audit. So you're best off hiring someone to handle both at once.

If you are hopelessly lost when it comes to financial matters in general, then your search for the right accountant is especially important. Look for an accountant who is truly interested in the way your studio operates, not just in tallying up the numbers at the end of the quarter. You may need a full-time adviser, and if so, you must be willing to pay for such expertise. An interested and helpful accountant can work with you on such tasks as keeping your studio's overhead costs down, writing a business plan (essential for planning expansion or applying for a business loan), and analyzing your cash flow (also important for helping you squeak by in lean times). His financial advice can produce savings that will more than offset his fees.

Your accountant should be a Certified Public Accountant (CPA) and be licensed with the state. Call your state's board of accountancy (listed in the state government listings of your yellow pages) to make sure that no complaints have been registered against him and that no disciplinary action has been taken against his practice.

Find an accountant who will take the time to explain accounting procedures to you and who will make sure you understand thoroughly any proposals for a new financial setup. If a CPA is "too busy" to explain, or claims the system or proposed change is "too complicated to lay out all the details," warning bells should go off in your head. The accountant is either lazy, inarticulate, dishonest, or some combination of all three. If you are to work well

PERSONAL PROFILE

BRUCE NADELL
Padell, Nadell, Fine,
Weinberger & Co.
New York, New York

"Accountants by nature are often precise, meticulous people. To find someone who can work well with your studio, you must look for a combination of creativity, absolute accuracy, and an ability to understand the particular problems of being paid for producing an artistic product. He or she must understand that designs are not widgets, turned out at a constant rate for the same costs and profit margins. That makes being an accountant for a design studio more challenging, but also more interesting," notes Bruce Nadell, partner in the New York City accounting firm of Padell, Nadell, Fine, Weinberger & Co. The firm has clients in all kinds of creative fields.

Mr. Nadell also stresses that because designers want to spend most of their time and energy on design work, not number crunching, they should look for an accountant who understands their abilities and specific needs. He advises, "Although you do want your accountant to work out creative ways to handle your studio's financial chores, you don't need someone who's going to design the most brilliant (and complicated) accounting system ever known to humankind. The system your accountant designs for you (or your bookkeeper) to use should be, first and foremost, *practical* and easy to use."

If you're looking to expand your studio's capabilities, or change or add to the types of clients you handle, your accountant should also be able to help you decide whether growth is wise right now from a financial standpoint. "Your accountant should see beyond the columns of numbers," says Nadell. "He or she should be able to look at the total picture from the financial angle while you look at it from the design angle. After all, both viewpoints are key in making a smart business decision."

with an accountant or financial adviser, it is essential that you both understand what is going on. In the end, you are accountable for the bottom line; make sure you get clear information in a timely manner so you'll be able to make informed business decisions.

You should also choose an accountant for your studio who has worked in your town for several years. Many states and cities have rather intricate tax laws, and you're better off with an accountant who's had plenty of experience with them. Don't pick a new person in town who must learn the hard way—at the expense of *your* studio!

Take the time to quiz any accountant you may be considering hiring to see how familiar he is with the design business. Does he understand how you are paid, and for what? Which seasons may be slow and why? That the business is extremely labor intensive and usually involves a fairly small capital investment? If he is to provide you with expert financial advice as well as a financial plan for your studio, he'll need a good working knowledge of the design business.

Ask any accountant you are considering hiring for a list of three to five clients you can contact as references. Ask specifically for references who are in the design field or in businesses similar to design so you can judge how well this accountant deals with creative people. Prepare a list of questions to ask when you call. (For example, ask whether the accountant was able to set up a simple, workable bookkeeping system for their business and whether they have a regularly scheduled review of the business's finances with the accountant). Check these references carefully. Because few designers have the know-how to check whether a CPA really knows his stuff, you'll probably need to depend a great deal on what others have to say about him.

Even if you are lucky enough to find someone who seems to handle your finances competently, you should still keep an eye on the books. If you dump the responsibility solely on your accountant, you are leaving room for simple misunderstandings and even fraud. Moreover, a working knowledge of how the money comes in and goes out can help you make key decisions, such as whether or not to take on *pro bono* projects for the exposure rather than the money, or whether or not to incur debt in order to buy new equipment.

FINDING A BANKER WITH YOUR INTEREST AT HEART

Your studio should have a banker or bankers, not just a bank. With deregulation of the banking industry, competition has gotten stiffer for all kinds of banking customers, and the image of the tight-lipped bank president in a three-piece suit, shaking his head "No" at you has almost vanished. You can now expect *service* from your bank.

The first people to ask for recommendations about which bank to choose are your lawyer, your accountant, and your local contacts in the design field. Your accountant in particular has probably had dealings with most of the banks in your area, and can let you know which he has found most satisfactory. It is also possible that your accountant has a professional relationship with officers in a certain bank, and this relationship can be of great help to you if and when you decide to apply for a business loan. After all, who better to vouch for your studio's profitability than the person who keeps track of the books *and* is friendly with the bank's loan officers? For these reasons, your accountant's advice on which financial institutions to choose can be invaluable.

If you've had a good experience with the bank that has your personal checking and savings accounts, consider using it for your business accounts as well. You stand a better chance of getting interested, satisfactory service if they know you keep all of your accounts with them.

Look for the smallest regional bank that has a wide enough range of services to handle your studio's account. Besides commercial banks, you might also consider credit unions and savings and loans. The smaller the bank, the more it will need your business, and the better service you are likely to get. As with many things, in dealing with a bank it is often better to be a big fish in a small pond than a minnow in an ocean.

As many people learned in the savings and loan crisis of the late 1980s, you should always check the health of a financial institution before letting it handle your studio's money. Deposits in most banks are insured to $100,000 by the federal government, but anything above that is at risk (although so far the government has *de facto* guaranteed accounts of all sizes at failed institutions). Even though you're insured, if your bank goes belly up, collecting on the insurance can take time.

To avoid such headaches, be sure to check any financial institution's solvency with your state's banking commission (listed in the yellow pages). If the bank is nationally chartered, contact the Comptroller of the Currency (202-287-4265) and the Board of Governors of the Federal Reserve System (202-452-3946). If you're not sure what type the bank is, call its customer service line and ask who regulates it. A good rule of thumb is to avoid financial institutions whose capital-to-asset ratio is less than 6 percent or whose after tax earnings are less than 1 percent of its assets. These numbers are public information and can be obtained either from the bank itself or the state regulatory agency for the banking industry.

To shop around for the most suitable bank for your studio, set up a hypothetical business account for your studio (using real dollar amounts) and ask each bank what services it could provide to meet your studio's needs and what it would charge for these services. For example, with several thousand dollars in savings and checking, writing thirty checks a month, and linking a company credit card to your accounts, ask what the various charges would be—for example, per check charges, annual credit card fee, flat monthly charges if your balance sinks below the minimum, and interest on a checking balance. Comparing the services and charges at several banks should give you a good framework for judging a bank's relative willingness and capability to handle a small business account.

But money isn't everything. Look for the small touches that can save your studio big headaches and you time or embarrassment: automatic overdrafts to cover checks with insufficient funds, one-day clearing for business-to-business checks, and other such considerate touches.

Another important factor in choosing the right bank is the banker. You should be assigned a specific bank officer who will address any problems or questions you may have with your account. In general, the longer a banker has been with the bank and the more experience she has in the business, the more valuable an asset that banker will be to your studio, especially if you apply to the bank for a business loan. If your banker is a known and respected officer of the bank and she endorses your loan application, the bank's board is likely to approve the loan more easily. The downside of having an older bank officer, however, is that since they have spent most of their careers in banking when it was heavily regulated, they may be less likely to bend the rules to better serve your studio.

While low fees and a bank officer's clout are important, also check potential banks for the efficiency and care with which they treat their customers. Can you reach the right people by telephone with relative ease when you have a problem? Are lines long or tellers surly? When you are shopping around for a bank and the bank employees know it, expect royal treatment, and be wary if you don't get it. Remember that time is money, and time wasted in long bank lines will cost your studio profits.

HOW TO FIND A DEPENDABLE BOOKKEEPER

Before you even consider hiring any kind of bookkeeping assistant, you should understand the books yourself. Work with your accountant to set up a system you can understand, and get a few months' experience using the system before you choose someone to hand the job over to. After all, if you don't understand the system yourself, how can you monitor a bookkeeper's effectiveness?

Depending on the size of your studio, you will want to hire either a part-time bookkeeper who comes in once a week or so, or you'll want a full-time person to act as bookkeeper and handle other clerical chores for your business. The kind of person you'll need also depends on your ability and willingness to handle certain tasks. Before interviewing candidates, be clear in your own mind about what you will expect from them: creative solutions to cash flow problems and an active interest in your designs, or just the ability to total the week's receivables and keep accurate records? Obviously, certain people are better suited to one type of work than the other.

Often your accountant or bank officer can suggest a good part-time bookkeeper. Some accountants even prefer that you use a bookkeeper that they already know and trust. So, for recommendations, go first to the person who must read your financial records carefully and work closely with the person who keeps them. It is imperative for the well-being of your studio that you find someone you can rely on and trust.

And trust is no small matter in these situations. If an errant bookkeeper embezzles studio money or botches your recordkeeping so badly that you end up with an IRS audit—be it caused by ineptitude, dishonesty, or both—his actions could cripple your design studio. If you are hiring someone who was *not* referred to you by a trusted friend, colleague or your accountant or lawyer, make sure to do a thorough check of his previous employer references and personal background. The worst mistake you can make is to assume that because you "don't have a head for business," all bookkeepers do. Just as there are good designers with integrity and poor designers with questionable ethics, there are bookkeepers of all sorts, and you'll need to put in some effort to find an able, honest one.

If you plan to hire an overall business manager rather than just a numbers-cruncher, you may want to ask other designers for recommendations. Look for someone who understands the *business* of design—someone who can price jobs, write contracts, track projects, provide clients with itemized estimates and set up a payment schedule, develop a filing system, and keep time sheets and records of the progress on different jobs. If you like to handle promotion and marketing yourself and deal with clients personally, fine, but if you consider that just another part of the business end of your studio, hire a business manager with skills in those areas as well. And while solid organizational and financial skills should be your first concern in hiring a business manager, it helps if you can find someone who has some design experience as well, especially if you plan to have your business manager handle such tasks as pricing jobs and tracking costs for your clients.

Like a good accountant, a competent bookkeeper should be able to explain to you fully and clearly where the money is coming from, going to, and has gone. Don't let financial mumbo jumbo act as a smoke screen for inept or dishonest dealings—if you don't understand something your bookkeeper or business manager is doing, have him or her outline it until you do. Or hire someone who can explain the accounting method more accurately.

If you hire a part-time bookkeeper who just comes in periodically, you should be getting someone who is *over qualified*. The finances of most studios are fairly simple, and any good freelance bookkeeper should have experience with businesses much more complicated than yours. If you have a doubt about a bookkeeper's ability to handle your finances, give the job candidate a bookkeeping test. You can find a model test (including the answers) in most elementary accounting books.

Your best bet is usually to hire a bookkeeper at a fixed monthly fee rather than paying him or her by the hour. In general, your bookkeeping needs won't vary much from month to month, but you'll want to feel free to call the bookkeeper with questions or have him or her spend extra time when need be. Your accountant should be able to give you an idea of the going monthly fee for a studio of your size in your area.

WHEN A CONSULTANT CAN HELP YOU

Most design studios can't run without some help from outside consultants. Whether a consultant handles a new marketing plan for you, finds you new studio space or renovates your current studio, develops a job-estimating or client-billing system, or analyzes your studio's workflow and makes staffing recommendations, you'll need to hire the best expert you can afford.

But before you hire anyone, pinpoint the problem as best you can by yourself. Sometimes you may have an exact idea of what you need, but in other situations you may have just a vague sense of the problem. In the latter case, before hiring someone to help you fix the problem, you should put some effort into understanding it yourself. Contact other design studios, your accountant and your attorney for their input on what *they* would do if they were in your shoes. You want to be able to give the consultant as concrete an idea as possible of the precise situation he or she must address. Otherwise, the consultant won't be able to discuss potential solutions in concrete terms, and you won't be able to gauge the potential effectiveness of her proposed solutions.

After you have a sense of the scope of the problem, ask colleagues and friends to recommend someone. You might also try the Small Business Administration office near you for a list of consultants in different fields.

Once you have a list of candidates for the consulting assignment, conduct an interview with each one. Résumés, degrees or certification should be looked at briefly, but what you are chiefly interested in is a candidate's *demonstrated* history of success. You will be paying for results, and that's what you should get. Ask each candidate to provide you with a list of satisfied former clients who can vouch for his or her abilities.

When you contact these references, don't just ask if the consultant was satisfactory. Call with specific questions: What did this consul-

PERSONAL PROFILE

EMILY COHEN
Graphics Business Consultant
New York, New York

"One of the most important aspects to look for in any consultant you hire is her ability to *customize*," says Emily Cohen, a business manager/consultant to such New York City graphics studios as Lloyd Riff Design Group, Ruth Ansel, and Jennifer Clark Design. "Instead of barging in and trying to make your studio run *her* way, she should listen, and then tailor her advice to improve—not override—your way of doing things." Cohen herself is a graphic artist, but she enjoys handling the business aspects of design for other studios that need her help.

"Every designer who hires a consulting business manager does so for a slightly different reason. Some people need help tracking jobs or keeping time sheets, others want advice about how to estimate expenses or send clients monthly statements. You'll work best with any consultant if you try to pinpoint what you need and then find the right person for that task. For instance, if marketing your designs is a weak point, don't hire a terrific job-pricer and overhead cost-cutter. Look for someone who can get your designs to the right clients," says Cohen. "It may sound simplistic, but some people are so lost when it comes to any aspect of running their studio besides creating designs that they hire the first consultant who comes along and seems to have some business sense."

Cohen also suggests choosing a consultant who will tell you what she *doesn't* handle well, and will suggest someone else for those tasks. She notes, "When people see that I have design experience and good business sense, they often dump every business chore in my lap with relief. I then have to tell them that they are wasting money in asking me to handle such things as bookkeeping when they could get someone else to do them at a much lower hourly fee than my rate."

tant do for you? Was the work done on time? Creatively? Thoughtfully? Did she go above and beyond for your company? Did she pleasantly surprise you? Were the consultant's work habits and rates agreeable? Keep in mind that you want to hire someone whose expertise is extremely valuable. You'll pay a bundle, so you'll want a superstar, not just an acceptable candidate. However, don't hire someone who is extremely *over qualified*—her expertise will cost you more than the use you will make of it.

In the interview, keep the conversation focused. Don't let a consultant use up all the interview time tooting her own horn; the last thing you want is a consultant who thinks she knows the answers before she knows what the questions are. Instead, talk about your studio, the specifics of the job at hand, and your objectives with this project. For instance, if clients have been complaining that they don't understand exactly what they are paying for, and you're interviewing potential consultants to help you set up a cost-tracking system, give candidates the real facts of your last job and ask them how they would suggest tracking the costs for billing purposes. If a response is vague or inappropriate, that consultant is probably not for you.

In a second stage, you might want to ask your top two or three candidates to submit a short, written proposal that details how they would approach your studio's problem. The care and creativity a consultant puts into such a proposal is often a telling indicator of how well she will handle the job, and how much she wants it. If a consultant is "too busy" to put together a carefully considered proposal, she may very well be too busy to handle your studio's problem effectively.

An important indication that you've got a good candidate for a consulting job is if she asks as many questions about your studio as you do about her expertise and qualifications. While you don't want someone who knows very little about the design business, you do want someone who is interested and involved enough to take a real interest in your studio's problem, even at the interview stage.

CHAPTER NINE
TROUBLESHOOTERS

Q. *I hired an accountant to straighten out my studio's tangled finances and set up a system I can live with. She's done a good job, but I'm still a little leery of paying the flat, per-month fee that she requested. Shouldn't she be billing me by the hour instead?*

A. As long as the flat fee is itemized so you can see exactly what services it covers each month, you're probably better off paying your accountant this way than by the hour. There are two reasons. First, this helps amortize your accounting costs over the entire year, rather than socking you with large tax preparation bills in April and at the end of the year. But more importantly, a flat fee makes your accountant more of a consultant and less of a simple numbers-cruncher. You should feel free to call her with any problems you encounter, or even to ask simple questions like whether your studio is eligible for a tax deduction you happened to read about in yesterday's paper. Paying an accountant a flat fee should help make her a trusted advisor rather than just someone who checks the books.

Q. *When I decided it was time to design a new self-promotion brochure for my studio, another designer recommended a well-known marketing consultant. I contacted the man and was impressed when we met over lunch, but he told me that submitting a written proposal was out of the question because he was too busy. Should I have contracted for his services?*

A. It's very hard to say, but it could be you saved yourself from making a costly mistake by not contracting with him. This man is probably a terrific marketer, but the question is, could he have designed a great promotional campaign for *your* studio? The fact is that you would have had to hire him without knowing specifically what he could do for you. It's probably better to choose someone willing to focus on your particular needs in order to get the job, even if he has less of a reputation as a world-class pitchman.

Q. *I had a contract dispute with one of my clients that ended up in court. The court battle was long and fruitless, and I wound up several thousand dollars poorer. Now that I look back on the incident, I'm not so sure I should have sued at all. Should one seek a "second opinion" before deciding to sue?*

A. That's not a bad idea. Even better, before you start a relationship with any attorney—even if you plan to use him only to look over contracts and such—check his record of litigation and cases won. Believe it or not, in most cases the best thing a lawyer can do for you is keep you *out* of court. When an out of court settlement may be possible, the last thing you want is for your studio to end up footing the bill while your attorney plays Perry Mason.

CHAPTER NINE
CHECKLISTS

To determine what kind of professional help your studio needs:
- [ ] Take a survey of your own skills.
- [ ] Know what you can't or shouldn't handle yourself.
- [ ] Don't try to "do it all."

Most designers need:
- [ ] An attorney.
- [ ] An accountant.
- [ ] A bank officer.
- [ ] A bookkeeper or business manager.
- [ ] Consultants of various types, such as a real estate broker, and marketing consultant.

To find the right attorney:
- [ ] Ask colleagues or the SBA for recommendations.
- [ ] Schedule an initial consultation with three or four attorneys.
- [ ] Go to the meeting with questions and pertinent financial information about your studio.
- [ ] Look for an attorney who is:
  - —A good small business specialist who understands the design business.
  - —Accessible and easy to communicate with.
  - —Able to recommend a good accountant, banker, and other contacts.

Look for an accountant who:
- [ ] Has the title CPA.

- [ ] Has a clean record with the state's board of accountancy.
- [ ] Will handle your taxes as well as regular accounting tasks.
- [ ] Will set up a simple bookkeeping system that you can follow.
- [ ] Understands the design business and can explain financial dealings clearly.
- [ ] Has experience with local tax laws.

How to find the right bank and bank officer:
- [ ] Ask your attorney, accountant, and local colleagues for recommendations.
- [ ] Consider using the same bank that handles your personal accounts.
- [ ] Choose a smaller, regional bank.
- [ ] Check the health of any financial institution with government agencies.
- [ ] Set up a hypothetical business account and compare charges and interest rates.
- [ ] Look for special services and courtesy.
- [ ] Request that a particular bank officer handle all of your affairs.

To find the right bookkeeper:
- [ ] Know your own bookkeeping system before hiring anyone.
- [ ] Decide whether you want just a bookkeeper or someone equipped to make business decisions and recommendations.

☐ Ask your accountant first to recommend a good bookkeeper.

☐ Do a thorough check of a candidate's previous employers.

☐ Hire someone who is able to clearly explain all financial transactions for your studio.

☐ Give candidates a bookkeeping test.

☐ Pay your bookkeeper a flat monthly fee (rather than paying by the hour).

Find the right consultants by:

☐ Pinpointing the problem you want to address before interviewing consultants to deal with it.

☐ Asking colleagues or the SBA for recommendations.

☐ Checking each candidate's degrees and certification.

☐ Asking for proof of a consultant's *demonstrated* success from satisfied clients.

☐ Questioning a consultant's references closely.

☐ Focusing the interview questions on your studio, not a consultant's achievements.

☐ Looking for a consultant who asks many questions about the project during the interview.

☐ Requiring candidates to submit short, written proposals for the project.

RESOURCES

Here are some organizations and publications that you can turn to for help in running your business.

ORGANIZATIONS

The American Arbitration Association
140 W. 51st St.
New York, NY 10020
212-484-4000

American Center for Design
233 E. Ontario, Ste. 500
Chicago, IL 60611
312-787-2018

American Collectors Association
4040 W. 75th St.
Minneapolis, MN 55435
612-926-6547

American Institute of Certified Public Accountants
1211 Ave. of the Americas
New York, NY 10036
212-575-6200

The American Institute of Graphic Arts
1059 Third Ave.
New York, NY 10021
212-752-0813

Artists in Print
Fort Mason Center
Building D
San Francisco, CA 94123
415-673-6941

Center for Small Business
Chamber of Commerce of the United States
1615 H St. NW
Washington, DC 20062
202-659-6180

Copyright Office
Library of Congress
Washington, DC 20559
202-287-9100

Federal Trade Commission
Washington, DC 20580
202-326-3175

Graphic Artists Guild
11 W. 20th St.
New York, NY 10011
212-463-7730

Insurance Information Institute
110 William St.
New York, NY 10038
800-221-4954

Internal Revenue Service
950 L'Enfant Plaza S., SW
Washington, DC 20024
Federal Tax Questions: 800-424-1040
To Request Tax Forms: 800-424-3676
For Recorded Information: 800-554-4477

Lawyers for the Creative Arts
220 S. State St.
Chicago, IL 60604
312-987-0198

National Small Business Association
1604 K St. NW
Washington, DC 20006
202-296-7400

Small Business Administration
1111 18th St. NW
Washington, DC 20036
202-634-4950

Society of Illustrators
128 E. 63rd St.
New York, NY 10021
212-838-2560

Society of Photographers and Artists
Representatives
1123 Broadway
New York, NY 10010
212-924-6023

Society of Publication Designers
25 W. 43rd St.
New York, NY 10036
212-983-8585

PUBLICATIONS
Books:
The Artist's Friendly Legal Guide
by Floyd Conner et al.
North Light Books, 1991

The Book of Small Business Checklists
by John Melchinger
The John H. Melchinger Company, 1989

Business and Legal Forms for Graphic Designers
by Tad Crawford and Eva Doman Bruck
Allworth Press, 1990

Clients and Designers
by Ellen Shapiro
Watson-Guptill, 1989

The Entrepreneur and Small Business Problem Solver
by William A. Cohen
John Wiley & Sons, 1990

Getting Started as a Freelance Illustrator or Designer
by Michael Fleishman
North Light Books, 1990

The Graphic Artist's Guide to Marketing and Self-Promotion
by Sally Prince Davis
North Light Books, 1991

The Graphic Artists Guild Handbook of Pricing and Ethical Guidelines
North Light Books, 1991

Hiring the Best
by Martin Yate
Bob Adams, Inc., 1988

How to Be Organized in Spite of Yourself
by Sunny Schlenger and Roberta Roesch
Dutton, 1991

Legal Guide for the Visual Artist
by Tad Crawford
Madison Square Press, 1990

Licensing Art and Design
by Caryn R. Leland
Allworth Press, 1990

PROMO 1
by Rose de Neve
North Light Books, 1990

Magazines:
How
F&W Publications
1507 Dana Avenue
Cincinnati, OH 45207
212-531-2222

Minding Your Own Business
P.O. Box 348
Newton Centre, MA 02159-9998
617-969-0823

Step-by-Step Graphics
6000 North Forest Park Drive
Peoria, IL 61614
309-688-2300

Success Magazine
342 Madison Avenue
New York, NY 10173
212-503-0700

INDEX

Improve your skills, learn a new technique, with these additional books from North Light